CAREERS IN CHILD CARE

CAREERS IN
CHILD CARE

By
MARY BOWMAN-KRUHM, ED. D.

The Rosen Publishing Group, Inc.
New York

Published in 2000 by The Rosen Publishing Group, Inc.
29 East 21st Street, New York, NY 10010

Cover photo © Jacques M. Chenet/CORBIS

Library of Congress Cataloging-in-Publication Data

Bowman-Kruhm, Mary.
    Careers in child care / by Mary Bowman-Kruhm.
       p. cm. — (Careers)
    Includes bibliographical references and index.
    ISBN 0-8239-2891-8 (lib. bdg)
    1. Child care—Vocational guidance—United States. 2. Child care—Vocational guidance—Canada. I. Title II. Careers (Rosen Publishing Group).
  HQ778.63 .B68 2000
  362.7'023'73—dc21

                                  00-028005

Manufactured in the United States of America

Dedicated to my daughter, Bonnie Redmond, and the staff, students, and parents of Community Montessori School, Herndon, Virginia.

About the Author

Mary Bowman-Kruhm, Ed.D., is a writer and faculty associate at Johns Hopkins University School of Professional Studies in Business and Education. She is also a contributing editor to *Children's Book Insider* newsletter. Bowman-Kruhm has authored, or co-authored twenty-five books with Claudine G. Wirths. *I Hate School: How to Hang In and When to Drop Out* was named by the American Library Association on its Best Books for Young Adults—1986 and Recommended Books for Reluctant Young Adult Readers—1987 lists, and by the National Council of Teachers of English in Books for You (recommended under Self-Help and Easy Reading categories).

For younger children, she has authored nine beginning readers in the Rosen A Day in the Life of... series. A picture book, *Busy Toes*, was written with Claudine G. Wirths and Wendie Old under the pen name C. W. Bowie.

In addition, Bowman-Kruhm is the author of numerous articles and stories in professional journals and magazines as diverse as *VOYA* and *Vegetarian Times*.

Acknowledgments

Thanks to the following for their help, information, and insights: Michelle Belski, April Blaney, Robin Brooks, Sydney Gurewitz Clemens, Carol Corbett, Layla Elkabli, Karen Haslett, Stephannie Ledesma, Cindy Lenzi, Joni Levine, Pam Main, Jimi Naccarato, Deana Preston, Bonnie Redmond, Denese Snell, Karen Sweeney, and Kim Unda.

x

Contents

Introduction

PICTURE YOURSELF . . .

Would you find satisfaction in a job in which you:

- Tie paper plates on your feet and those of a group of children and slide across the floor?
- Talk with a child who is sad because her grandmother has died?
- Help a child work on a messy art project without doing the work for him?
- Take children on a walk to find wildflowers and write a poem about those you pick?

If so, a job in child care may be right for you.

IS THIS CAREER FOR YOU?

Would you apply for a job if the ad read like this?

Wanted: Person to do a job that requires long hours of work. Low pay. Little public appreciation. Many frustrations.

Many people would not. Yet every day those who work in the child care field happily go to work because they feel the rewards and benefits outweigh the negatives mentioned in the ad. These are people who choose to work with young children.

The key word is *choose*. Those who successfully work in child care love young children and have a

1

strong desire to help them grow to their full potential—physically, intellectually, and emotionally.

IN THIS BOOK

This book will help you decide if your desire to help young children is strong enough to make child care your career choice. In Part I you will discover the qualities needed for success.

In Part II you will look at the wide range of jobs open to you. You will read about salary, training needed, how to get started, and points to consider. You will meet people who work in a variety of jobs in different child care settings:

- Becky, a nanny
- April, a family care provider
- Kim, a teacher assistant
- Karen, a teacher
- Jimi, Denese, and Layla, a teaching team at a Montessori school
- Bonnie, a director of a school
- Stephannie, a tutor in a hospital

Part III will help you prepare for a child care position, find the right job, and take your first steps in your chosen career.

Throughout this book you will see some of the challenges and problems of a career in child care. You will also see how rewarding this career can be to someone who chooses to work with young children.

PART I

WHY CONSIDER CHILD CARE?

1

Qualities for Success

IS A CHILD CARE CAREER RIGHT FOR YOU?

If you're thinking about a career in child care, here are a few questions to consider:

- Do you like to baby-sit and would you like to work in child care by having a regular babysitting job?
- Are you willing to work hard but do not want to go to college?
- Do you want to know how you can take care of children in your own home?
- Are you unsure what you want to do career-wise but know you enjoy working with small children?
- Do you want to know more about work in a special area of child care, such as teaching music or art, or working with children in a hospital?

Although many jobs in child care are available and waiting to be filled, working with young children is not right for everyone. The chart that follows can help you decide if a career in child care is right for you. It lists areas that are important for success in a child care job. You don't have to mark a firm "Yes" for all of them. If you hope to do a good job and feel a sense of success, however, most of your dots should be close to the left side of the chart.

Is a Career in Child Care Right for You?

Put dots on the checklist at the places that show your answers to the questions. Then look at where the dots fall.

- If your dots are almost all on the left side of the checklist, child care is a field for you to consider.
- If your dots are mostly in the middle or to the right, another career field may be the best choice.

	Yes	Not Sure	No
Are you in good health?	☐	☐	☐
Would you like to be with children all day?	☐	☐	☐
Are you willing to work in partnership with parents?	☐	☐	☐
Are you able to speak clearly?	☐	☐	☐
Can you write clearly and concisely?	☐	☐	☐
Can you accept all children, including those with problems?	☐	☐	☐
Are you willing to:			
• Learn about child care resources in your community?	☐	☐	☐
• Take courses in child development and first aid?	☐	☐	☐
• Continue to learn throughout your career?	☐	☐	☐
Can you work as part of a team?	☐	☐	☐
Do you act in a mature way in stressful situations?	☐	☐	☐
Can you respond quickly and calmly to emergencies?	☐	☐	☐
Are you able to break down jobs into small tasks?	☐	☐	☐

Do you respond to children:	Yes	Not Sure	No
• in a warm, loving way?	☐	☐	☐
• in a way that encourages them to problem-solve?	☐	☐	☐
• with a focus on positive behavior?	☐	☐	☐
Can you meet a child on his/her level?	☐	☐	☐

Are You in Good Health?

Working all day every day with small children requires a huge amount of energy. As part of your daily tasks, you will sit on the floor, sing and dance, help children put on their outdoor clothes before taking them outside, and be responsible for the well-being of many children. When the day is over, you plan for tomorrow. To be successful in this high-energy job, a child care provider's body has to be in great shape and he or she must be willing to face each day with enthusiasm.

Would You Like to Be with Children All Day?

Children go through different stages of development as they grow. A two-year-old is not like a three-year-old or a four-year-old. Children at these ages differ in what they can do and say, in the way they play, and in the way they relate to other children and adults.

Even with their differences, most children ages two to five can be described as full of energy, funny, independent, curious, adventuresome, inquisitive, self-confident, assertive, smart, persistent, loving, excitable, enthusiastic, playful, longing to please, affectionate, entertaining, and sometimes frustrating.

If these qualities excite and delight you, then a career in child care may be equally rewarding.

Are You Willing to Work in Partnership with Parents?

A career in child care, however, doesn't stop with working with children. You will also talk to and work with parents. Your attitude toward the parents matters a great deal. When you talk with parents, remember that their reasons for leaving their child with you are private and personal. Your job as a child care provider is to accept their child and help him or her to the best of your ability.

Parents who entrust their child to the care of someone else for the first time need your support. They care deeply for their son or daughter and for their child's well-being, and they are often afraid and confused by the new world of child care they are entering. How you respond to them can help them feel at ease. They need to be constantly reassured that their child will be happy and safe under your care.

On the other hand, you cannot take on the role of parent. You are the child care provider. The parent rightfully decides the number of hours the child will be with you each day and makes choices about special diet, clothes, and any other needs for their child. You can tactfully provide input, but final decisions belong to the parent.

Are You Able to Speak Clearly?

Ability to speak well is important. You may be talking to parents who have a different background from yours. Often you will talk to them on a daily basis, even if only to say a few words about how their child's day went.

When you speak to parents, especially about difficult subjects, you will need to be tactful. For example, if a child misbehaves, the parent needs to know. The two of you may need to problem-solve about when the poor behavior begins (day of week and time of day), what triggers the behavior (someone or some event at home or with you), and what should be the consequences of that behavior.

Can You Write Clearly and Concisely

Your ability to write is also important. Many centers require that notes documenting daily activity for very young children be given to the parent each day. Most children above the age of three take a note home on a weekly basis. The notes may be in the form of a checklist and usually include a few personal words.

At centers, accidents and bad behavior also need to be written up, both for school records and for parent information. Writing is needed that is fair, clear, and to the point, without the use of name-calling or strong words that will upset the reader. Spelling and grammar are important, too. If you are caring for the child at home, you should keep a log that describes each day's events.

Can You Accept All Children, Including Those with Problems?

You must be able and willing to treat all children equally. All children have needs. All children have strengths. The strengths and needs of some children are more easily seen than those of others. A child care worker's job is to build on each child's strengths while helping him or her with their needs.

Are You Willing to Learn?

As a child care provider, are you willing to:

- Learn about child care resources in your community?

8

• Take courses in child development and first aid?
• Continue to learn throughout your career?

High school courses in child care are desirable. Post–high school training is both desirable and often required by local law. Even if courses are not required, a good child care provider must have a desire to learn more about how children develop, why they act as they do, how to keep them safe, and how to help them learn and grow.

Can You Work as Part of a Team?
Since a nanny or family child care provider takes care of children in a home, parents are the only adults with whom they work. In centers, however, most people work as part of a team. A teacher assistant and a teacher are often in each classroom and all staff unite and work together to help each other. They share ideas, provide support, solve problems together, and jump in to help when an emergency arises.

Do You Act in a Mature Way in Stressful Situations?
Children are often kind and loving but many can sometimes be unkind. You cannot take things they say personally. You are the adult and you must help them understand what they did or said and help them grow from the experience.

Parents may also say things that upset you. Even if responding in an objective way is hard, you must remember that you are the child care professional.

Can You Respond Quickly and Calmly to Emergencies?
If a parent storms into the school and begins to yell at his child, what would you do? If a girl hits another child

over the head with a large toy truck, what would you do? If a child has a seizure, what would you do?

Right now you may not know the best way to deal with each of those situations. But you must remember to stay calm when difficult situations arise. You should be able to move quickly to protect the child or children and either handle the problem yourself or send for help.

Are You Able to Break Down Jobs into Small Tasks?

Helping children carry out activities requires breaking down a large job into small tasks. The directions you give children can have only one or two steps. You have to wait until the first steps are carried out before moving on to the next step. For example, you might first tell children to put away their toys. Then you could tell them to get their jackets from the hook and put them on. After that has been carried out, you could tell them to line up to go outside.

You also have to break down the activities you plan into small segments and think through what might happen at each step. For example, if you put too much paint in a cup, it is likely to spill. If you give the children the choice of too many colors, they may mix them together to make a ghastly shade of brown. Remember, what's obvious to you is not always obvious to them.

How Do You Respond to Children?

You must still have a bit of child inside that you allow to come out when working with children. If you remember how much fun dancing around a room, wearing a costume, or playing tag can be, a job with very young children may be the right job for you.

Can You Meet a Child on His or Her Level?

The job of working with children requires finding joy in childhood. You must love children and be able to respond to them in a way that makes them feel comfortable.

FUTURE TRENDS

As we begin the twenty-first century, we are starting to see trends in the field of child care:

The movement of women into the workforce means most families need child care on a daily basis. The September 1999 issue of *Covering Child Care* reports that, "Nearly two-thirds of all American mothers are working, and child care has become a fact of life for millions of children." Surveys show about the same percent of Canadian families needing child care.

The quality of care children receive varies widely, but much of it tends to be poor. The summer 1999 issue of *The Children's Beat* reports that, "As the century turns, the majority of young children are in child care and much of it is not very good."

Growth in public and professional awareness. Thanks to the media, the public is more aware of child care as an issue. Television programs have focused on preschoolers and the needs of families. Membership in professional groups has blossomed and Internet bulletin boards and Web sites link families and child care staff.

Funding. Public awareness has, in turn, influenced funding. State and local funding and support are currently high.

Even with increased awareness, the public does not view child care as a right that children need and deserve. The public does not even agree that child care is right for children. Most people see care for young children as a personal family problem. They fail to recognize that money spent on child care today is an investment in the well-being of tomorrow's teens and adults.

Child care workers are paid poorly and benefits seldom exist. People seem quick to praise child care professionals. However, in a society in which money reflects power and prestige, they are still slow to compensate them. Child care jobs continue to be some of the lowest paying jobs, with salaries less than almost any other type of work. In 1996, the U.S. Bureau of Labor Statistics reported that median weekly earnings of full-time child care workers were $250. Animal caretakers who worked full-time in 1996 earned $290 each week. In other words, those who provided care for animals earned 16 percent more than those who provided care for children.

In September 1999, *Covering Child Care* reported that, "Child care workers are virtually on the bottom rung of the occupational ladder, according to the Census Bureau, with wages that have fallen over time . . . and then remained stagnant."

The Impact of These Trends on You

What do these trends mean for you, as someone who is thinking about a career in child care?

Jobs will be plentiful. The *1998-99 Occupational Outlook Handbook* of the U.S. Bureau of Labor Statistics lists child care workers as one of the jobs predicted to have the largest growth. Growth between 1996 and 2006 is projected to be 36 percent.

Pay, however, is poor and will probably not get better in the near future. Most parents who pay for child care simply cannot afford a steep increase in fees. Public money is needed if pay is to increase to a level equal to that of public school teachers.

People's attitudes about who is responsible for child care do not seem to be changing very quickly. Some people feel that the public schools do not educate older children well, so why turn early childhood education over to them? Others feel the responsibility belongs to the parents. Many people simply do not see the education of young children as crucial and worthy of public funding.

In the meantime, parents in Canada and the United States struggle to find the best care they can afford for their children who cannot yet care for themselves.

2

How Children Grow and Learn

A child care provider spends much of the day assisting children as they carry out activities to help them learn and grow. These early years in a child's life set the stage for the person that child will become. In any child care job, the goal is to help children reach as far as each is able and become independent. To achieve this goal, an understanding of how children develop and learn is needed.

HOW CHILDREN GROW

Research points to the following factors about how babies and young children grow:

- Most children move from one milestone to another in similar ways. They begin creeping when they are about six months old. They progress to crawling, then walking, and—by age two—to running. Ability in other skills follows similar patterns.

- Children vary from each other and reach different stages at different times. One child may not be able to catch a ball at age three; another child the same age may catch a ball very well. But the first child will probably learn to catch as he moves closer to age four.

- Windows of time seem to exist in which a child is most open to learning a particular concept. A baby who does not receive love and does not feel secure in his early months may have trouble connecting closely with others in later life. A child who does not hear many words spoken in the first few years of life may have a limited vocabulary when he or she grows up.

The Five Fields of Growth

A child grows in five areas. These are:

- Cognitive
- Language
- Physical
- Emotional
- Social

Our brain influences all of these areas. We cannot talk or move or think without our brain talking to the rest of our body and telling it what to do.

Although the brain continues to change during a person's life, it grows fastest during the first three years of life. The way we feel, think, and behave begins to develop at this time. As the brain grows, the child grows in each of the five areas.

Cognitive

Cognitive, or mental, development refers to the ability to think, reason, and learn.

Babies and toddlers grow cognitively by using their senses to explore. They see, hear, taste, feel, and smell the world around them in order to understand how it works. Young children also learn when adults show them how to do something and then let them do it, such as feeding themselves or watering a plant. Teachers call these experiences "active, hands-on learning."

As toddlers grow to be young children, they learn from interacting with the world around them. For example, a child putting together a puzzle can learn both by doing things correctly (putting pieces in the right places) and by making mistakes (putting pieces in places where they don't fit). An adult, watching the child with the puzzle, may say the child is playing. Adults often forget that children learn from play. Play to an adult means fun and games. Play to a child may be fun, but it also helps them learn and grow cognitively.

Language

A child's development of language use is important because people use language to express their thoughts and ideas. Listening and speaking are skills that help children learn to read and write when they enter school.

Because the use of language is so crucial in our society, parents and teachers are often concerned about a child's ability in this area. As with other areas, however, growth occurs in stages. And individual children progress at different rates, going through each stage at the pace that is right for them. It is important to make sure that each child completely experiences and learns each step before he or she is asked to move on to the next one.

Physical

Physical development includes skill in using muscles required for activities such as throwing, running, and jumping. It also includes skill in using muscles for cutting, drawing, and buttoning. Being able to use fine motor skills is a necessary part of a child's total muscular development.

Emotional

Emotional development deals with children's feelings. Research in both the United States and Canada suggests that a negative caregiving style that ignores a child's emotional needs can result in poor behavior by the child or a drop in intelligence. There are many other reasons a child may have emotional difficulties, but this research needs to be noted by child care providers and parents alike. Emotional problems can impact the child socially.

Social

Social development refers to getting along with others. Lillian G. Katz, an expert in the field of child care, reports, "Evidence has been accumulating for more than twenty-five years—primarily in North America—that unless a child achieves minimal social competence by about the age of six, plus or minus a half year, the child is at risk for the rest of his or her life."

Watch how clever some children are at socially adapting what they say and how they act. A four-year-old may say to her mother, "Can I have a drink before we leave, please?" To her little brother she will say, "Want to go bye-bye?"

ONE AREA OF DEVELOPMENT INFLUENCES THE OTHERS

Development in one area influences development in the others. For example, a child whose language is delayed often suffers from social problems because they can't communicate well. Being teased or rejected by other children may make the child feel bad about themselves and thus affect the child's emotional well-being.

READINESS FOR KINDERGARTEN

The pattern of growth in each area varies a great deal from child to child. One child may have good small motor skills and be ready to learn to tie her shoes. Another child may still need help pushing his foot into a shoe.

It's helpful to know skills that most children have by the time they enter school. The list below is not meant to be complete but only to give examples of the skills most children should have.

- Cognitive: Count to ten, name body parts, name colors, understand the concept of danger (high places, hot stove, traffic), remember a song or nursery rhyme

- Language: Talk in sentences that can be understood by strangers, follow simple directions, use words to express thoughts, print or recognize their first name

- Physical: Can use the toilet by themselves, hang up clothing, bounce a ball, go up and down steps

- Emotional: Accept small disappointments and not cry, play by themselves, enjoy and not fear new activities

- Social: Play with friends, take turns with toys and with playground equipment, sit quietly while listening to a story

INCLUSION

Some children are not able to achieve the level of skills their preschool peers do because of a disability. A child, for example, may have cerebral palsy (CP). CP is caused by a brain injury that affects a person's ability to control his or her muscles. CP can be mild or severe. It may impact one, some, or all parts of the body. Someone with CP may have trouble moving and talking but may be equal to peers in the cognitive area.

Most child care programs now include one or more students with disabilities, which is called inclusion. In the United States, federal laws mandate inclusion. Canada has been moving toward inclusion without these laws. Students with disabilities may have a variety of conditions that hinder their progressing at the same level and in the same way as other children their age. Being with other children, however, gives them the best chance for long-term success in life.

The most common long-term condition is a learning disability (LD). A learning disability is a disorder that causes a person of average or above-average intelligence to have greater difficulty with reading, writing, math, listening, thinking, or talking.

Two other disorders are related to LD:

- **Attention deficit disorder (ADD).** A student with ADD has trouble paying attention and focusing on a task.

- **Attention deficit hyperactivity disorder (ADHD).** A student with ADHD has trouble paying attention and focusing on a task and is also overly active. He or she acts before thinking about the results of the actions.

ADD and ADHD are not the same as LD. Some specialists consider them a form of LD. About 20 percent of students with learning disabilities show some form of

ADD or ADHD. All three of these disorders can range from mild to severe.

Working with parents and specialists, including the child's doctor, is necessary during the preschool years if a child is overly active. Techniques to manage the child's behavior should be carefully tried over time by both parents and child care providers. Anyone who is with the child regularly each day may need training in these techniques. Only if such techniques fail should medication be used. Before using any medication, however, the parent must consult the child's doctor.

WHY QUALITY CHILD CARE MATTERS

Most parents recognize how important their children's development and learning are in their early years, and they struggle to make a good child care choice. Research supports their need to choose wisely.

In 1998, RAND, a research group, reviewed a number of studies on child care programs and noted long-term gains in certain areas. These include:

- Emotional or cognitive development for the child
- Improvements in education; for example, less need for special education
- Increased economic self-sufficiency, first for the parent and later for the child, through work efforts, higher income, and less use of welfare
- Less criminal activity later in life

This report and similar studies support the research of Lillian Katz, who suggests that "what we do with and for children today is related to all of their tomorrows."

3

Child Care Settings

The public tends to think of child care as a service that allows parents to work. Most parents, however, see child care as a way of meeting the needs of their children.

Parents in the United States and Canada can choose from among several types of child care settings. The type of care they choose is often determined by the amount of money they can afford to pay.

THE THREE TYPES OF SETTINGS
The settings in which paid, formal child care is provided in North America fall into three main types, with each type broken into different groups. These types are:

- Care within the child's home
- Care in a family child care provider's home
- Care in a center

Care within the Child's Home
People who care for children in the child's home as a career go by a variety of names. Each name carries with it a slightly different job description and different responsibilities.

- **Baby-sitter:** Provides care for children on a full-time or part-time basis. No special training or background required.
- **Au Pair (pronounced *oh pear*):** A foreign

young person, usually between the ages of eighteen and twenty-five, who lives with a host family for a year or so. He or she receives a small fee in exchange for taking care of the children. An au pair joins in family activities. May have some background working in the field of child care in their own country.

- **Nanny:** May live in or out of the home. Main job is to care for children. Does household chores related to caring for children. Experience and training may be little or great. Age eighteen to senior citizen.

- **Governess:** Usually has a college degree and provides at-home schooling for children who are school age. He or she is a teacher and is not involved with care of younger children.

The government does not regulate paid positions within a family home. The family is responsible for interviewing and hiring the person they feel can best meet the needs of their children.

Care in a Family Child Care Provider's Home

The setting for care by a family child care provider is the provider's home, rather than the child's home. In Canada, this type of care is also called other-home care. The child care provider may or may not be licensed. In many areas, licensing, and the regulations that go with it, is based on the number of children in the care of the provider.

While licensing does not provide a guarantee of the quality of care, it does mean the safety of the home has been approved and someone other than the parents deems the environment a good one for children. A licensed caregiver is, in most states and provinces, required to have taken classes in child development and first aid.

CARE IN A CENTER

Center care is also known as day care. Professionals seldom use the term because it can be confusing. First, many people believe day care is simply baby-sitting. Second, the term itself can refer both to care in a private home (family care provider) and care in a center. *Nursery school* and *preschool* are other terms less used today. They often refer to half-day or part-time programs.

The two types of care within a center are:

- For-profit: The center is run as a business to earn a profit.
- Not-for-profit: Centers which are run by a government agency, a group (or cooperative) of parents, or by a place of worship are usually not for profit.

For-profit centers include nationally known chains of centers, such as La Petite Academy and KinderCare Learning Centers. These centers are often franchised, which means they are run according to the guidelines and standards of the chain but run by a local owner. For-profit centers can also be only a single center or a small group of centers in a local area, usually run by someone within the community.

Head Start programs across the United States are a prime example of not-for-profit care funded by the federal government. Many local governments in both the United States and Canada fund their own centers. The U.S. military provides service personnel with child care through a group of centers located around the world.

Many places of worship sponsor child care in their building during the week. These are usually run on a not-for-profit basis. Although these centers provide a general program, they also introduce children to basic religious concepts. Many parents feel that learning these basic concepts teaches young children values and lays the groundwork for better understanding of a particular faith when the child is older.

Companies often have centers on site. Many companies believe that parents may do a better job and take less time off if child care is not a problem for employees who are parents. Centers operated at a place of work may be either not-for-profit or for-profit.

It is important to remember that the quality of care children receive cannot be measured by whether the center is run on a for-profit or not-for-profit basis. No matter what type, all centers must be licensed and usually have some staff with formal training in child care.

TYPES OF PROGRAMS IN CENTERS

If the setting in which you prefer to work is a center, you need to consider the types of programs that center emphasizes. Each center develops its own curriculum.

Many centers build their programs around a set of guidelines developed by the National Association for the Education of Young Children (NAEYC) and the National Association of Early Childhood Specialists in state departments of education. These guidelines state:

- Children learn best when their physical needs are met and they feel safe and secure.

- Children learn when they are actively involved with people and materials.

- Children learn through social interaction with adults and other children.

- The way children learn reflects a recurring cycle of awareness, exploration, inquiry, and utilization.

- Children learn through play.

- Children's interests and need to know motivate learning.

- Each child varies in his or her pattern, timing, and style of learning.

DAP

Centers that follow the above set of guidelines carry out a program that is called Developmentally Appropriate Practice, or DAP. Developmentally Appropriate Practice means matching learning activities to each child's stage of development. What the child is able to do is more important than his or her age. A child of three, for example, may be ready to click the computer mouse so she can play a game that matches sounds with letters. Another child of three may not yet understand that sounds make up language. This child may also need to develop his or her fine motor skills before he or she is able to use the mouse.

Not everyone agrees with DAP. Those who agree with DAP feel that a program should be *learner-centered*. Those who disagree feel it should be *learning-centered*, which means that the child should, based on their age, meet certain standards and the focus should be on academic achievement.

J. E. Stone, writing in *Education Policy Analysis Archives*, says that DAP "has encouraged parents and teachers to be less assertive and to afford children greater freedom." According to Stone, because of DAP, parents do not insist that their children study and work hard. He also believes parents tolerate poor behavior. He speaks strongly for "educationally appropriate" instruction, which expects students to meet recognized standards and to reach higher levels of academic achievement.

Centers with educationally appropriate curriculum base their programs on the belief that a child's brain develops much more in the first few years of life. Because of this, they believe young children need a strong academic program to take advantage of those prime learning years. These centers offer a program with courses similar to those found in the higher grades such as music, foreign language, math, and computer work, but which are geared for younger children.

The debate between DAP and educationally appropriate programs is not a simple one. As parent and public concerns about quality education mount, the argument seems to be heating up. The NAEYC feels the issue should not be turned into an either-or proposition. They believe children should learn in a variety of settings.

In fact, many centers offer a curriculum that incorporates ideas from each of these methods of teaching. Instructors introduce the children to academic learning, but they also allow time for free play and play with the other children. They allow the children to grasp academic concepts when they are able.

WHAT DOES THIS MEAN TO YOU?

Each setting or program offers strengths and features that are right for certain children. Just as a parent must find the right place for a child, someone who works in child care needs to find the right setting or program for their own career satisfaction.

4

Special Schools of Thought

SPECIAL PROGRAMS

The owners, directors, and staff of many centers strongly believe that certain methods can best help the children under their care. These methods come from a philosophy, or set of beliefs, about early childhood education. Three programs followed by a number of centers in the United States and Canada, as well as elsewhere in the world are:

- Reggio Emilia
- High/Scope
- Montessori

The Reggio Emilia Approach

The Reggio Emilia approach is named after the small town in northern Italy where it began. This approach to childhood education has many features that make it an outstanding approach to early childhood education, including:

- An emphasis on developing expression through many techniques, such as art—using various media, such as clay, paint, chalk—acting, music, and writing

- An open setting that encourages children to interact with one another

• An emphasis on projects in which a class or small group of children investigates a topic in depth

According to Lillian Katz and Sylvia Chard, both experts in the education of young children, the greatest contribution that the Reggio Emilia teachers brought to the child care field was the use of extensive documentation of children's activities and behavior. It is now a standard part of classroom practice.

According to Katz and Chard, "Documentation typically includes samples of a child's work at several different stages of completion; photographs showing work in progress; comments written by the teacher or other adults working with the children; transcriptions of children's discussions, comments, and explanations of intentions about the activity; and comments made by parents. Observations, transcriptions of tape recordings, and photographs of children discussing their work can be included. The documents reveal how the children planned, carried out, and completed the displayed work."

This thorough recording of a child's progress contributes to the child's learning in a number of ways. For example:

• When children see evidence of how their work has improved, they tend to work harder.

• Teachers plan activities that are appropriate for the children because they are aware of each child's strengths and needs. They also avoid repeating activities. Instead, they will choose a variety of activities that use many types of media.

• Parents like to see the progress a child is making.

The High/Scope Approach

The High/Scope approach uses guidelines that are based on research of how the brain functions and how children learn. The emphasis in the High/Scope approach is on "active learning," a form of education in which children learn through interacting with other adults and children.

High/Scope programs emphasize four areas:

Room Arrangement. A High/Scope classroom contains materials and equipment that are located in special interest areas. Examples of such areas are those for books, art, and house play. Everything is labeled and is within easy reach.

Daily Schedule. A day's schedule seldom changes, so the children know what to expect.

Plan-Do-Review. Children plan their activities, do them, and then reflect on what they did and the results.

Key Experiences. Teachers do not directly teach skills, but provide materials and help students have experiences that lead to learning. Lists of developmental behaviors for each child help teachers plan activities and talk with parents about their child's work.

High/Scope was originally a program for children at risk of school failure. The High/Scope preschool approach is now used in public and private child care programs, Head Start programs, and home-based child care programs. Research has been so favorable that the methods of High/Scope have expanded into many settings with all types of children.

The Montessori Method

The beliefs of Maria Montessori are followed in more than 5,000 schools around the world.

According to Tim Seldin, the president of the Montessori Foundation and the chairperson of the International Montessori Council, you can find them "in a church basement, perhaps a converted barn, in shopping malls, former public buildings, and some buildings specially designed for Montessori programs. There are programs in Harlem, migrant workers' camps, and on Indian reservations. These hearty souls live and breathe their work, creating wonderful intimate communities that radiate a sense of personal attention and family."

Maria Montessori started her first school in Italy in 1907. She believed learning should occur in multi-age classrooms. She believed that children in various stages of development would learn from each other. She preached Developmentally Appropriate Practice long before the term was developed.

Many teachers with Montessori training carry Maria Montessori's ideas into their classrooms in schools not allied with Montessori. Teachers who follow Maria Montessori's ideas base their teaching on three strong beliefs:

- **Education for young children needs to be child-centered.** This means classroom furniture must fit the child, and materials and equipment must be easy to reach. Although learning is aimed to appeal to children as fun and playful, it is, at the same time, intended to help children learn and grow cognitively.

- **The teacher acts as a guide to help the child be successful.** A teacher is not someone who gives facts to be memorized and insists a task be done their way. Their job is to guide the children to learn and figure things out on their own.

- **The child should learn at his or her own pace.** Children should not feel pressured to learn academic skills. A child should have time to master a skill without being rushed or pushed. On the other hand, a child, when ready, can move on.

"Montessori is a 'thematic' approach to education, in which we focus our entire studies around one given theme or topic at a time, and involve the entire curriculum in looking at it from many perspectives," Seldin says. "When we study China, we look at the land itself, the climate, the plants and animals that live there, the people and their housing, food, dress, lifestyles, stories and legends, art, music, dance, and celebrations. The fact that almost all of our teaching involves direct hands-on experiences makes us almost unique within contemporary education."

Because Maria Montessori's beliefs have had such a huge impact on the field of child care, let's visit a typical Montessori school.

MEET DENESE, LAYLA, AND JIMI

From 9:20 to 9:45 AM, during circle time, the students in Denese Snell's classroom talk about the date, the day's activities, and the weather. Individual lessons begin at 9:45. From Monday through Thursday, this independent work continues until 11:30 AM. Denese works with each student during this time. This personal or small group learning time—there are no more than three students working with the teacher at a time—for about ten minutes, is a hallmark of any Montessori program.

Since Montessori education is hands-on learning with a purpose, some of the students use special Montessori materials. One student works with a bead frame that resembles an abacus. The bead frame helps students move from the concrete to the abstract in working with numbers.

Another student is being introduced to decimals, although she doesn't know it. She is working with beads strung on wire to make up bars of ten, squares of one hundred, and cubes of one thousand.

Based on the Montessori philosophy that children enjoy activities and items that are teacher-made, teachers put a great deal of work into making and collecting their own equipment and materials.

One student hammers golf tees into a box filled with clay. Another student shines shoes. Still another student is tweezing grains of dried corn from cobs into a bowl. The corn will then be given to birds to eat. Whether teacher-made or Montessori-endorsed, all materials allow the children to learn by doing, and nothing—not even a grain of corn—is wasted.

The school administrator, Bonnie Redmond, says, "Montessori stimulates the children and keeps them busy. I've never seen a child unhappy with learning in a Montessori school, even if it's someone who has special needs."

During this individual learning time Layla Elkabli, the teacher assistant, rotates around the room and monitors the other children. She does not, however, do more than keep the noise level down and help the students. A Montessori-trained teacher does all actual instruction.

Layla's family believes so strongly in the Montessori approach to child care that her granddaughter is a student and her daughter is also a teacher assistant at the school.

On Fridays, the curriculum changes with individual lessons ending early. Then, Jimi Naccarato, a Montessori teacher from another classroom, works with the group on singing and movement. Denese moves to Jimi's room to work with his students during this time.

As Jimi sets up his electric keyboard, each child puts away the game or activity he or she was using. The children also roll up the mats on which they had been sitting during their learning time and store the mats in a box. Then they sit cross-legged on the carpet, behind the yellow tape that outlines the circle area.

Jimi rolls his hand down the keyboard to announce he's ready to begin. During the next half hour the children sing, dance, and move to Jimi's direction. To their delight, they finish by pretending they're whales. As Jimi strikes a low note, they wriggle and wiggle across the sea floor.

The children go outside for a half hour and then eat lunch. Lunch is provided by "satellite," which means a company prepares the food off-site and brings it to the school in large trays.

After lunch, children under the age of five nap while the kindergartners return to an instructional program. The rest of the day is spent playing with games and reading books. The children also have one more outdoor recess period because the Montessori system teaches that activities out of doors are a very important part of a child's development.

At the end of the day, teachers must make sure everything is in its place on the shelves. But true to Montessori philosophy, the children pitch in to help. "We teach grace and courtesy the first six weeks of school. This sets the routine for the school year," Bonnie says.

FINDING OUT MORE

In the back of this book, Appendix A, "Information about Child Care Organizations and Training Programs," gives contact information to help you find out more about each of the three philosophies.

If you feel you would like to work in a school like one of those described in this chapter, visit a local school that adheres to those beliefs. You may be allowed to visit classrooms or you may only be able to meet with the director.

No matter what job you have in child care, all three of the programs described in this chapter present a sound philosophy of early childhood education. The programs they offer may not be right for all children and may not be right for everyone who works in child care. Experience with any of them, however, will be helpful in your future career.

PART II

THE CHOICES

5

Nanny

If your view of a nanny comes from what you have seen in the movies or on television, life as a nanny may not seem like a serious career. But it is.

A nanny is responsible for the care of the child or children in the employer's home. Although nannies play games, and wipe noses, and wear casual clothes, they are professional in their attitude toward their job. Their job is to work in partnership with the parents to provide care for the family's children.

MEET BECKY

On September 23, 1998, First Lady Hillary Rodham Clinton presented the 1998 *Parents* magazine Child Care Award to Becky Kavanagh. Now president of the International Nanny Association, Becky was happy to answer some questions about a career as a nanny.

Q: Why did you choose a career as a nanny?
A: My background is in early childhood education, with work in group child care centers and preschool programs. I had set a professional goal of spending several minutes each day in a personal way with each child. After seven years I knew the disappointment of not achieving that goal on a daily basis. So when a friend told me about a family interested in securing private child care for their growing family, I opened myself up to the possibility that this might be a refreshing new challenge to embark on. Once I met the family, I knew that this was for me.

Q: What are the most important issues to discuss prior to accepting a new position?
A: I feel there are several things that must be discussed thoroughly during the interview process: special expectations (meal preparation, visits to doctors, errands, children's activities, and so on), discipline philosophies, approximate daily schedule, compensation package, household guidelines, and religious or cultural expectations.

To me, however, the most important issue throughout the process is the chemistry between the nanny and the family. It is a difficult thing to describe, but vital in the relationship that is being formed.

Q: What are some of the best things about being a nanny? And some of the worst?
A: For me the best things far outweigh any negatives. Knowing that you can make a difference in a child's life, contributing to the parents' productivity at their job by providing a positive environment for their child, and feeling the love of a child as someone special in their life are only a few of so many positives.

Isolation from other adults can be a challenge as can working longer hours (often nannies work a nine to ten hour day). Self-motivation, flexibility, and dedication to purpose are musts for thriving in a nanny career.

Q: What is your daily routine like?
A: As the children grow and develop, the daily routine changes. I have been with my current family for ten years now. I've seen the children change from the infant and toddler stages to school age. When they were younger, much of our schedule was set around feedings and naps.

There would be opportunities throughout the day for active and quiet play, along with story time, art, music, and snuggling. As they each matured, additional activities that met with their interests were added to the schedule (preschool classes, sports, music lessons, etc.).

In addition, we opted to homeschool the oldest child until eighth grade. It was an experience that I thoroughly enjoyed. She is a very gifted student and needed more of a challenge than a regular classroom could provide.

Now with all the children in school, I have time to volunteer in their classrooms and become more involved in their special interest groups, such as Girl Scouts, Cub Scouts, dance, and music.

Q: How do you feel about video surveillance?
A: Our society today is filled with cameras taping us. Many large companies use some surveillance, as do stores, malls, and some child care centers. I understand parents' desire to be sure their children are completely safe at all times. The building of a strong relationship between parents and caregiver requires trust. Therefore, if a family is considering video surveillance, they should discuss this up front with the nanny prior to the nanny's accepting an offered position. That way everyone is clear, and if the nanny is strongly opposed, he or she has the option to refuse the position.

Q: What does the future hold for the in-home child care industry?
A: I believe that more families will choose private care in their home in the future. Parents are seeing that investing in their children by employing a nanny provides

many benefits. The flexibility that the family gains is a real benefit, particularly with very young children because it allows them to sleep in their own beds, be cared for when they are ill, and have a daily schedule based on their own needs and interests. With a nanny, an in-home child care consultant is available to the family.

GETTING STARTED

Anyone over the age of eighteen can begin a career as a nanny. Many young adults entering the field foresee a lifelong nanny career. Others are young people who want a nanny position for a year or two as a break from another job or from college. Other nannies are much older. They have either reared families and want to continue to work with young children or have had a career in another field.

A job as a nanny offers lots of choices. If you are thinking about being a nanny, here are some questions you should consider before you start your job search:

- Do you want to work full- or part-time?

- Do you want to live outside or in the home of the family?

- Do you want a job that lasts several years or one that is temporary? Some nannies who like change specialize in taking on temporary work.

- What type of relationship would you prefer with the family? Some families happily include the nanny as a family member. Other nannies are treated as an employee.

Nanny jobs can be found by word-of-mouth referrals, by notices on community bulletin boards, and through newspaper ads.

One of the most reliable places to get a job, however, is from a nanny placement agency. The family, not the nanny, pays the agency. These agencies screen applicants and try to match the strengths and skills of nannies with the needs of families who apply. The parents then interview possible nannies and do the actual hiring.

If you are interviewed in the family home, you will get a sense of whether working with the family will be a good match. Many families interview twice, so do not be surprised if you are invited to return for a second interview.

Other tips for beginners:

- Consider a job as a summer or short-term nanny. This will give you an opportunity to see if you really enjoy the job. You will also have some great experience to put on your résumé.

- Investigate such groups as the International Nanny Association and the National Association for the Education of Young Children. Information about both of these and other child care groups can be found in Appendix A.

- Read child care books and take classes, especially first aid and cardiopulmonary resuscitation (CPR).

- Visit a library or bookstore and become acquainted with children's literature, especially picture books. Both libraries and bookstores often have helpful people who can direct you to books children especially enjoy. In many places, lists of age-appropriate books are available.

POINTS TO CONSIDER

The family for whom you work may be very different from your own. You may take a job far away from your own family and in a community very different from yours.

You will hear personal things from the children and the adults in the household that you must not repeat, unless, of course, the children are in danger.

You must also support and teach the family's views on rearing children. When you disagree about certain ways of handling a situation, you must be willing to talk honestly with the parent about your feelings.

Even if you are only thinking about a temporary career as a nanny, look over the points below to help you better understand what such a position involves. If you are offered a job as a nanny, return to the list and discuss each point with the family before you agree to accept the position.

- **Hours to be worked and days off.** Hours per week range from forty to sixty, with two days, typically weekends, off.

- **Pay.** How much and how often?

- **Length of probationary period.** The period of time needed to tell you, the children, and the parents if the match is a good one.

- **Job evaluations.** When and how often your work will be evaluated.

- **Job responsibilities.** Include preparing meals, planning the amount of learning activities to be included in the daily routine, type of discipline, driving, visits with child's friends at friend's home and family's home, and so on.

- **Household work.** Usually related to care of children.

- **Baby-sitting.** Pay or extra time off to compensate for staying with children in excess of regular work hours.

- **Living arrangements.** Private bedroom and bathroom. Meals and other food.

- **House rules.** Guidelines to cover assorted situations, including your being ill, telephone calls (while you are caring for children and long distance calls at any time), your visitors and guests.

- **Paid holidays and personal leave days.**

Many nannies and parents work out and sign a written agreement. You can find sample agreements in child care books and on the Internet or, using the above list, you can write your own.

Although it may seem strange, you may want to discuss issues about leaving your job. Leaving a nanny position can be harder than leaving most other jobs. Since nannies often become part of a family and have fewer children in their care than most child care workers, leaving has an impact on everyone—the nanny, the parents, and the children.

SALARY RANGE

Salaries range from $300 to $600 weekly, based on training, hours, benefits (health insurance, sick and personal leave days), and location. A live-in nanny usually has a private room and bath and often the use of a car.

Nannies must pay taxes on their salary and are entitled to benefits, including credit for the employer's share of social security.

TRAINING NEEDED

Although many families do not require more than a high school education, courses in CPR and first aid, as well as other related training, are important. As with other child care jobs, the more training you have, the better you will do on the job and the more money you will be able to earn.

General child care courses at local community colleges are usually the least expensive way to gain training. If you are still in high school, taking classes in family life or child development is also very helpful.

Special nanny training programs are also available. Depending on the program, training ranges from six weeks to a year and may include working with young children in a lab-type setting. See Appendix A for more information.

PLEASE NOTE

The future looks bright for anyone wanting a position as a nanny. According to the International Nanny Association, "In 1997, nannies cared for more than three million preschoolers in homes with working parents. That number has nearly doubled since then."

In Canada, according to the Toronto *Globe and Mail*, approximately 127,000 children are cared for in their home by nonrelatives (nannies). It also reported that Canadians often prefer family-type child care to care offered by centers.

6

Family Child Care Provider

Many people, mostly women, find that caring for children in their home is rewarding work, especially if they themselves have young children. Parents often prefer to have their child cared for in someone's private home. Care in a home is the preferred option of parents in Canada where it is also called other-home care. The goal of these caregivers is to create a warm, loving home away from home for the children.

MEET APRIL

Every weekday morning April Blaney welcomes five children into her home. They join her own three children for the day.

April acts as a loving mom, not just a caretaker, for all of the children she cares for, and her home reflects her concern for them. A special large, airy room is well stocked with games, books, and toys for young children of all ages. Although she works with the children on colors, shapes, and letters, and involves them in lots of activities, she does not consider herself a teacher. April feels strongly that, for ages four and under, quality care and love are more important than academics.

April laughs at being called a stay-at-home mom because she is on the move a lot. Each day she navigates her car to drop off and pick up children and to take short trips with the group under her care. She often picks up children at the homes of their friends and drops older siblings at school.

She also tries to do the kinds of things she would do if she were home during the day with her own children. A trip to the library or zoo with eight children, however, means piling out of the car, getting the two smallest into a double stroller, and matching a younger child to an older buddy for safety.

GETTING STARTED

April began serving as a family child care provider when her oldest son was born. She realized she would be happiest if she could care for Robert herself, so she decided to check out state and local laws that would allow her to be paid to care for children in her own home.

April considers the job of caring for children in her home a career and a business. If you feel the same way, licensing is crucial. Many home caregivers elect not to be licensed. They provide care on an informal basis and, in doing so, leave themselves open to many possible problems, including lawsuits. Having a license also tells parents that you treat the care of children seriously and it shows professionalism.

The first step is to check out state, or province, and local laws that deal with caring for children in your home when the children are not members of your family. Depending on the state or province, requirements will vary.

Many places have regulations based on the number of children for whom you want to provide care. April recommends applying for the maximum number possible, as a family may want to place several children with you. Oftentimes, your own children count in the number you're allowed.

Obtaining a license can take a long time, sometimes up to a year. For April, the process to get her home approved and obtain the needed licenses took almost six months and a great deal of work.

Both she and her husband, Michael, had to be fingerprinted and have a criminal background check. April's entire family had to have complete physical exams. They are obligated to have these exams every two years.

The home had to pass a thorough inspection. In order to maintain their license, they must pass this inspection every two years. Luckily their home is on one level, with no stairs that could be a danger for toddlers. April said that having a new home on a single level and a fenced yard helped them get the permits they needed.

START-UP COSTS

April recommends that someone starting a family child care business have at least $500 set aside for expenses. The figure needed will vary a great deal, depending on what you need. If you already own equipment such as car seats and toys, your start-up costs will be fairly low. Other items, like a computer and software program for bookkeeping are convenient, but not always necessary for you to start your business. If you are on a tight budget, it is important to itemize the costs of those things you absolutely need and pass on those items that you can wait to have until your business is off the ground.

Count on having some unexpected expenses. April doesn't have city water. She was surprised when she learned she had to pay to have her well water tested. An inspection by the fire department was also needed. Together, those two inspections cost about $100.

WHILE YOU WAIT

While waiting to receive licensing approval, you can spend the time in a number of useful ways:

- **Get advice.** Talk to other home child care providers. Contact the office in your town or county that works with home providers.

- **Learn about the paperwork involved.** You may need help and advice to set up books, complete tax forms, and get insurance.

- **Develop a contract and fee structure.** Keep in mind that you are entering into a contract with the parents whose children will be in your home. You may want to develop a formal contract or you may simply want to list matters that concern both you and the parents. Such items include: illness you discover after a child arrives for the day, payment when the child does not attend, and items parents need to supply or items you will provide, such as extra clothes, towels, toilet articles, and food for special diets.

- **Purchase, prepare, and accumulate materials, supplies, and equipment.** Collect art supplies, empty boxes, used greeting cards, stickers, and so on. Yard sales and consignment shops are a wonderful source of used toys but much care must be given to assure that they are in safe and clean condition.

- **Ready your home.** Make a safe playground with outside toys and a fence. Prepare areas where children will play and eat. Decide what areas, if any, will be off-limits to the children. Can your own children keep bedrooms as havens of their own or do you need to use their beds at nap time? Consider storing some of their personal items and toys. Storage bins and shelves may need to be built.

- **Take classes.** While waiting, take classes such as first aid and cardiopulmonary resuscitation (CPR).

GETTING CLIENTS AFTER YOU GET APPROVED

Unless you have a list of waiting clients, you may want to contact an agency that refers parents to providers. These agencies may also provide other services, such as a newsletter, a Web site with information that will match providers with parents, and meetings on how to operate a child care business.

Other ways of advertising include flyers, newspaper ads, and notices on local bulletin boards. April has relied on word of mouth and has never had to advertise. Unless you live in a very remote area, you will probably have little trouble amassing the number of children for whom you are legally able to provide care.

POINTS TO CONSIDER

Because family child care providers contract with individual families, income may not be stable. If a family has several children in a home and there is a change in their situation, such as if they move or if one parent quits their job, the caregiver may be faced with a sudden and drastic loss of income.

Personal situations a family child care provider must take care of during the day also arise. For example, the child care provider can become sick or need an appointment with a doctor, lawyer, or other person who is not available at night. Finding someone to substitute for part of a day is sometimes necessary.

If a caregiver is absent for a day or longer, parents usually do not pay. Some providers, however, contract with the parents for sick leave and personal leave days.

Many family child care providers have split days that require special attention. For example, a parent may have a child who will be in your home in the morning but goes to kindergarten in the afternoon. That child's spot may then be filled by an older child who attends school during most of the day and then goes to the child care provider until the end of a parent's workday.

SALARY RANGE

According to a 1996 Child Care Bureau study, family child care providers have very low earnings. They earn $9,528 annually after expenses. Unregulated providers, who care for fewer children and are offered fewer supports, earned just $5,132 after expenses.

Why are earnings so low? Gross earnings may seem high if one multiplies the number of children by the amount parents pay each week. That figure, however, is deceiving, as many expenses are involved when taking care of children in a private home. Some items, such as food for lunches, are obvious and can easily be factored into a budget. A few expenses that are less obvious include:

- A car or van that will seat all the children

- Gas and wear-and-tear on the car

- Equipment such as car seats for younger children and cots or mats for napping

- Replacement of toys, games, and books

- Craft materials

- Replacing home items like carpeting, wallpaper,and washing machines because of excessive use

Utilities such as oil and electricity, insurance, and the part of a house used by the children may be tax-deductible. An accountant or tax adviser can provide details related to taxes.

THE TRAINING YOU NEED

The training needed to care for children in your home varies by state or province. Some areas require none; others require a specific number of hours. Many states require classes in child development, CPR, and first aid.

An accreditation process has been developed by the National Association for Family Child Care (NAFCC). This accreditation system defines quality standards for family child care and promotes training for providers. To learn more, see Appendix A, National Association for

Family Child Care or go directly to their Web site at www.nafcc.org and click on "Accreditation."

PLEASE NOTE

Many people choose to be a family child care provider because they want to work with children and prefer to work out of their home. Many, like April, have young children of their own. April says, "This is a great career for moms who want to stay home, at least until their own children enter school." It is a career, April says, that "allows me to supplement the family income and still be home with my own kids."

April also describes her own children as helpful, thoughtful, and willing to share. She credits these qualities in part to having other children in their home every day.

7

Teacher Assistant

Many child care teachers begin as teacher assistants. A teacher assistant may also be called an assistant teacher, educational assistant, teacher aide, instructional assistant, and even paraeducator.

The main duty of a teacher assistant is to help with the care of the children under the direction of the teacher. Many teacher assistants also do clerical work, such as keeping records, putting up bulletin board displays, and copying materials. Because teacher assistants often work part-time, it is an excellent job if you have other obligations during the day.

Many teacher assistants prefer being paid to work with a teacher in a classroom, which in many states and provinces counts toward certification. This on-the-job experience is great preparation for a future child care job. You'll see how all sorts of daily tasks are carried out. You'll learn how to discipline small children and how to organize their activities through hands-on experiences such as taking children on field trips. You'll learn the best ways to ask questions that make children think and the kinds of books young children love to hear read aloud. Because each center is different, you'll also begin to collect ideas about the different styles of teaching from the teachers with whom you work.

MEET KIM

Kim Unda arrives at WEE Center in Rockville, Maryland, after her morning classes at the local community college. The children at WEE Center are just waking up from naps. They say hello and greet her warmly. One boy always hugs her and says, "I love you, Miss Kim."

After she greets the children, she helps them put on their shoes and put their blankets away. Then the children wash their hands and prepare for their afternoon snack. Because this is a church-sponsored school, they have a short prayer before they eat.

After snack time, the children play for a half hour. Play is outside if the weather allows. Kim monitors their play and sometimes joins in to help keep games running smoothly or get sports equipment. When they come in from play, the children settle down in a circle to hear the teacher read a story. While the teacher reads, Kim calms fidgety children. When the teacher is absent, Kim takes over the reading and a substitute takes Kim's role.

The afternoon story has a religious theme that relates to the Bible. Each story stresses moral values rather than specific church doctrine. The stories are simple and easy to understand. In one story, for example, a man had dirt thrown in his eyes. The teacher stops before the end of the story and asks the children to predict what will happen. Then she reads the end of the story, which tells how he prayed and how his sight returned.

A planned activity follows Bible story time. This activity is either related to academic work or is an art project. If the activity is an academic one, the children might trace numbers or trace their names.

Collage is a favorite art project. Everyone does the activity to the best of his or her ability. Kim and the teacher help but insist the children do the cutting and pasting themselves. This not only helps children improve their fine motor skills but also helps them learn how to rely on their creativity.

An activity that involves art is often based on the topic of the week. When the topic was nutrition, for example, the children made collages of nutritious foods and then played a card game. For the game, each child picked a card with a picture of a food and put the card in one of two envelopes that were labeled "Healthy" or "Not Healthy."

At about 4:30 PM, it's "center time." In the play room there are all kinds of centers.

- A music center, at which the children use head-phones to listen to a cassette

- An art center, at which they draw or use Play-Doh

- A computer center

- A book center

- A housekeeping center with child-sized kitchen equipment

- A Legos center, at which they can make models using the interlocking plastic pieces

Each child picks what he or she wants to do and plays at that center for the rest of the afternoon. Parents start to pick up their children about 5:00 PM. Two staff members—a teacher assistant and a senior staff person—stay until all the children are gone.

Kim loves her work. Disciplining children, she says, is the hardest part of her job. None of the children are bad, but they occasionally get into quarrels. "When two kids hit each other and each blames the other," Kim says, "it's hard to know who is right, who is telling the truth."

Kim worked full-time at WEE Center during the summer. The summer program is less academic than during the school year and allows staff more freedom to carry out activities. Kim taught Spanish and cooking skills. She got books written in Spanish from the library and made up games, such as Bingo, that used Spanish words.

Although she will live on campus during her final two years of college, she hopes to substitute during long vacations and continue to work at WEE Center during the summers.

Kim's long-term goal is to become an elementary school teacher. She also hopes to get married and have children of her own. She feels that a career working with young children is the best possible preparation.

GENERAL DUTIES OF A TEACHER ASSISTANT

According to the *1998–99 Occupational Outlook Handbook* of the U.S. Bureau of Labor Statistics, half of all teacher assistants work part-time. Depending on their schedules and the hours they are needed, teacher assistants work various shifts during the day. Many centers open at 7:00 AM, and the last child leaves eleven or more hours later.

Duties are related to time of day. Most often teacher assistants take their lead from the classroom teacher. They help in whatever way the teacher wants and fill in with other center-requested duties. Generally, teacher assistants:

- Help with classroom activities

- Help with clerical jobs, such as copying, organizing field trips, and keeping attendance and health records

- Stay with the children while the teacher has a daily lunch hour and short breaks. May also cover the classroom for about an hour each week during the teacher's planning period

- Help children with special needs, such as changing diapers or toileting and feeding

- Clean the bathroom and classroom during the children's rest time

- Monitor children on the playground

- Help with center jobs, such as opening and closing the center, bus duty (if transportation is part of the program), and serving lunches and snacks

ADVICE FROM KIM

Kim feels anyone who works as a teacher assistant should "find joy working with children." She says she loves working at WEE Center and looks forward to finishing her college classes and going to work.

POINTS TO CONSIDER

Teacher assistants have a very physical job, and it can be tiring. They often work outdoors in all kinds of weather. When they are inside, much of their day is spent bending, standing, walking, and kneeling. They also occasionally dance, sing, and skip. Assistants who work with physically disabled students perform tasks that are even more strenuous. They may need to feed, lift, and toilet students.

The job is also emotionally tiring. Children can be demanding, and working with them is fast-paced.

GETTING STARTED

Despite the job demands, a position as a teacher assistant remains the way of choice to enter the field of child care. A high school diploma or its equivalent is required, but further education or training is seldom needed. The *1998-99 Occupational Outlook Handbook* of the U.S. Bureau of Labor Statistics notes that most training for child care workers is received on the job.

Look at your strengths. What skills do you have that would be helpful in working with young children? What experiences have you had?

Kim, for example, speaks Spanish. Her mother was a family child care provider, and Kim helped when her mother was sick or needed extra hands. She has also done a great deal of baby-sitting.

In the eleventh grade, Kim took a child development class. Young children from the community came into her high school, and Kim gained a lot of useful experience. "You not only teach the children but have a chance to observe and see how the children act and react to different situations. Our class was divided into groups and one group would teach, one would plan, and one would observe behind mirrored glass."

59

Not everyone can offer a center the extensive background Kim has, but everyone has many experiences and qualities that will be helpful in a job as a teacher assistant.

Make a list of all your strengths that might help you get a job and perhaps earn more money per hour. Dig deep and talk to people who know you well and can help you. Consider the following questions:

- Have you done volunteer work?
- Do you speak another language?
- Do you know any signs used by those who are deaf or hard-of-hearing?
- Do you have experience working with someone who has a disability?
- Are you organized?
- Have you traveled a great deal?
- Have you done clerical work for a teacher in high school?
- Do you baby-sit?
- Do you enjoy crafts and art projects?
- Are you a member—perhaps an officer—of a club or another group?

SALARY RANGE

Salaries vary a great deal, based on region, experience, and academic background. For beginners in the field, minimum wage is often the rule.

PLEASE NOTE...

The outlook for openings as teacher assistants is excellent. The *1998–99 Occupational Outlook Handbook* of the U.S. Bureau of Labor Statistics cites the position as one in which the need is expected to rise by 38 percent between 1996 and 2006.

8

Teacher

Child care centers are the type of care chosen by most parents who look beyond family members to find care for their child or children. In the United States, the National Center for Education Statistics reports that in 1995 more than half the parents who chose care outside the family selected center-based care for their three- to five-year-olds.

Meet Karen

Karen Sweeney teaches two-year-old children and, as Karen calls those who are slightly older, young threes. She works at La Petite Academy. Most days begin with Karen and her teacher assistant taking their thirteen children outside to play.

When they return to the classroom, Karen reads a story to the children and then they do an art activity. Karen plans art projects that are done by the children themselves—creative and messy but a real learning experience. Today the students are making a collage out of textured materials that Karen and her assistant have collected. According to Karen, two- and three-year-olds love to touch the various materials and glue them onto sheets of heavy paper.

Because the morning is prime learning time, at 10:10 AM the class begins work by talking about the calendar. As they talk about the month, day and date, and weather, Karen gives them little jobs to do, such as pointing to the day's date on the big calendar. "It makes them feel independent," she says.

Then the children move on to other learning activities that help them develop concepts. She works, for example, on counting and colors. She often reads a book and uses an educational board game, card game, or some other learning tool that the children can touch, handle, and play with to help them grasp a concept.

Each activity takes about ten minutes. It's important to keep the children moving through these learning activities quickly because they have short attention spans. They finish the morning by going outside again, weather permitting. The children then wash their hands and take turns setting tables before they eat.

Nap time follows lunch. After they wake up, Karen reads to the youngsters, and then they sing and dance and move to taped music. Karen says, "Hearing the children sing the songs I've taught them is one of the favorite parts of my job."

As the day winds down, the class enjoys free play. When parents arrive, the children give them the daily sheets Karen has filled out so that each parent has personal information about their child's day.

The day is fast-paced because, as Karen says, "I think it's important for the children to have a well-rounded background, doing lots of things." Although the structure of the busy day tends to keep discipline problems from happening, she does sometimes have to pull a child aside and talk to him or her.

Karen leaves only after she has tidied up her room and finished her paperwork. The paperwork required of a teacher takes a great deal of time. Any mishaps or accidents must be written up and so must anything out of the ordinary that Karen or her teacher assistant saw. If a child comes to school with bruises or cuts or burns, Karen must record and date that information, in case those injuries become part of a pattern to that child.

Many teachers love teaching but dislike paperwork. Some, but not all, programs require that almost everything be documented: attendance, meal counts, running logs of information about the children, and all parental contact. These parent contacts include both telephone calls and personal interactions. They may be casual chats or formal meetings. All need to be recorded if the center requires it.

Karen must also plan for the next day. Although she has used books from the public library to teach herself plan lessons (required by many states and provinces), the center where she works provides her with lesson plans. She often changes them to suit her students' needs but finds the packaged plans a great resource that saves her time and gives her ideas and activities to use in her classroom.

Karen is a true professional. She feels she is a good teacher because she has "patience and understanding with the children." She is willing to put in the hours needed to help her children have happy learning experiences.

GETTING STARTED

Find out what your state's requirements are for becoming a child care teacher. The reference section in your public library can help you, and you can phone government agencies.

You can also go on-line to check requirements. One Web site offering this information for the United States is the National Child Care Information Center at www.nccic.org. Click on "State Profiles" on its home-page. In Canada, a list can be found at Child Care Canada at www.cfc-efc.ca. Click first on "Child Care Connections" and then on "Directory."

Beginning as an assistant teacher is an excellent way to enter the field. Your work in the classroom will often count toward teacher certification. Tell the center administrator that you hope to become a teacher and want to work with a skilled teacher who will act as your mentor.

Take classes, even if your state's requirements for certification are few. Ask experienced teachers what classes they feel are most important. When you have completed the needed training, think carefully about the type of center in which you would like to teach. Each center has its own personality and its own beliefs about what makes a center successful for the children who are enrolled.

POINTS TO CONSIDER

A child care teacher seldom has a routine day. When asked why she liked her job working with young children, Pam Main, a Head Start teacher in West Haven, Connecticut, replied, "One reason is that it gives me the chance to do—and be—a little bit of everything. I cook, eat, read, go for walks, build snowmen and sand-castles, dance, mold clay, pet guinea pigs, watch fish swim, listen to music, have interesting conversations, hear jokes—all day long! Look at almost any book on staying young and vibrant. All of these things are on the list of suggestions."

Karen, however, warns, "Don't come in thinking teaching small children is all fun-and-games or baby-sitting. It's work."

Karen also suggests that if you are thinking of a career as a teacher, you should "work with all different age groups." She has worked with infants to children twelve years old and found she most enjoys those just leaving their toddler years.

Lastly, teachers in child care centers often work with other adults. Laws about the number of children with whom a teacher can work vary across the United States and Canada. Adding a teacher assistant increases the number of children allowed. Many teachers have at least one additional adult in their classroom. Karen says, "Respect the person you're working with. Don't think because that person is an aide that you're better than they are."

SALARY RANGE

Wages tend to be low and jobs offer few benefits. Only 18 percent of child care centers offer fully paid health coverage to teachers. Generally, teachers like Karen earn little more than the minimum wage, which in 1999 was about seven to nine dollars an hour in the United States and the equivalent in Canadian dollars in Canada.

Carol Corbett, the director of WEE Center, in Rockville, Maryland, says, "You have to have people who are motivated to work in child care by something other than take-home pay. There are trade-offs that people have to make in their lives to work in child care."

TRAINING NEEDED

Although salaries are lower, the education level of child care teachers is higher than that of the general population.

Training is often required to gain or renew certification. As with most jobs in child care, requirements, like salaries, vary greatly from state to state and province to province. The trend, however, is to require teachers to continue to take course work and training. In 1986 only thirty-three states required ongoing training for teachers. By 1997, forty-four states required ongoing training.

The need for training has received a big boost from two studies:

- The results of a 1998 study by the National Center for Education Statistics concluded that many parents today see a need for trained staff. Past studies have found parents were more concerned about the cost and convenience of care than about the training of their child's teacher.

- A review of worldwide research by the Association of Early Childhood Educators in Ontario, Canada, found that children cared for by teachers with training in early childhood education "show increased cooperation and social skills, more developed cognitive, language, and pre-mathematical skills and a more persistent approach to task completion."

Because of such research, course work by staff seems to be in the best interests of everyone.

Like many child care professionals, Karen takes more classes than those required by her state, including some at a local community college. She subscribes to *Early Childhood News*, which is sponsored by the University of Wisconsin-Stout, and gains credits through assignments that go along with articles. (See Appendix A.)

PLEASE NOTE

Training to get a job as a child care teacher seldom requires a degree from a college or university. Having a degree in early childhood education, however, offers you more job options. Required course work can be taken at local community colleges, and credits are often offered by local agencies and organizations involved in child care.

Jobs are widely available and the need for teachers keeps growing as more and more parents need child care while they work. Turnover is high, however, since many teachers leave for better paying jobs.

Poor pay is the single greatest problem for child care teachers. The responsibilities placed on a teacher are huge, yet pay is low. Many child care teachers, however, share Karen's feelings. She says she enjoys her job "because I see what a difference I make in the children's lives." Many people feel this kind of reward outweighs the low wages, high parent expectations, and heavy responsibilities.

9

Other Jobs Caring for Children

Most centers and family care providers open their doors to children from early morning to early evening. Even so, many families need care during late evening or night hours when children aren't able to attend a regular program.

According to *Flexible Child Care in Canada*, "Families sometimes have needs for child care which are not easily met by ordinary child care services. When a child is ill, when the usual caregiver is unable to provide care, or when other short-term child care emergencies arise, many families are unable to find care. Similarly, shift workers often find it difficult to make suitable arrangements for care for their children. Farmers and other rural workers often find it impossible to arrange reliable, convenient child care to meet their needs."

Finding child care that meets their needs is still a problem for many families. Opportunities are growing outside the traditional areas of child care, but you will probably have to seek out such jobs.

Consider the following positions if you are open to working in more specialized areas of child care:

- Teaching special subjects in a center
- Providing substitute and backup care
- Providing care during nontypical work hours
- Caring for young adults with disabilities in group homes

- Teaching children in hospitals
- Providing after-school care for older children

Other opportunities continue to arise. Some movie theaters and grocery stores are hiring staff to provide child care while parents enjoy a show or shop. You can also find part-time jobs as a camp counselor, a tutor, a helper in the children's section of the library, and even as a Christmas elf.

If You Have Special Talents
Someone who has a talent in a special field may be able to turn that skill into a part-time job. Combining several of these jobs could give you a full workweek and your own business.

Some child care centers hire part-time staff to provide instruction in:

- Art
- Music
- Foreign language
- Physical education or gymnastics

Again, you will need to seek out centers. You may want to volunteer your services or charge a low rate during a trial period.

Using Your Special Talents
If you are seeking a position in which you can use your special talent, you must also have a talent for teaching this skill at the level appropriate for young children. You cannot expect too much of them or accept too little. They will learn only if they are

69

actively involved at the level at which they can achieve their best.

Centers that hire someone to teach a special subject want someone who will provide creative instruction for the students.

Robin Brooks, an art teacher, says, "Even children as young as twelve months can begin to paint and draw. Thick unwrapped crayons give children a sturdy implement with which to draw. At this stage, drawing is scribbling, a largely physical activity. You can help a child by looking at their drawing with them and describing the variety of marks they have made: dots by banging, lines that go across, etc. You might also ask, 'How did you move your arm to make this line? Can you show me?' In this way, children will begin to see the connection between their motions and the marks they make.

"Many young children are eager to use a brush and paint to explore mark-making. You can write down what they say at the easel and copy their 'story' on a small card that can be displayed next to their drawing.

"As they get older, you can also gently guide them along by saying, 'You have done lots of around and around. How about trying up and down or side to side, fast, or slow strokes?' Painting is very physical and it involves many types of mark-making. The broader the repertoire a child has, the more easily she or he will be able to move toward creating symbols—people, places, animals, etc.

"I never cease to be awed at the process, especially when a child creates their first intentional symbol. Regular, repeated opportunities throughout early childhood to draw and paint freely give young children a foundation of experience that helps them become confident in their own creative selves."

SUBSTITUTE AND BACKUP CARE

Like all of us, child care workers get sick. As a result, substitutes in child care facilities, including family care homes, are in demand. The need for substitutes is so high that agencies have been created in some areas to help place people.

The pros and cons are those found in most substitute jobs: You can choose the places and dates you work, but pay is not regular.

CARE DURING NONTYPICAL WORK HOURS

Although local laws may restrict the number of hours a child can be cared for outside a home, some centers and private individuals provide care during hours when most centers are not open. In Whitehorse, Yukon, for example, Carol's Playcare Centre provides evening, overnight, and emergency child care in a twenty-four-hour center for a small number of children who participate in the regular daytime program.

If you are willing to care for a child with disabilities in the child's home, try contacting sources in your community. Start with the local Association for Retarded Citizens (ARC), schools that serve students with disabilities, and the offices of pediatricians who specialize in the care of children with disabilities. Tell them that you are willing to provide relief care for parents who want or need to get away but want their child with special needs to be well cared for. Parents of children with disabilities often contact those places for the names of people who are willing to provide relief care. Such jobs may also be listed in the newspaper.

CARE FOR YOUNG ADULTS WITH DISABILITIES IN GROUP HOMES

Meals and a place to live are often available if you would like a job as a house parent who lives in a group home. Religious groups and other organizations sponsor these homes. Groups that work with people with special needs, such as autism and mental retardation, also sponsor homes. The work with these young people may be demanding and the pay very low, but the experience can be rewarding.

Check newspaper ads and call local groups that work with people with disabilities if you are interested in such a job.

TEACH CHILDREN IN HOSPITALS

Children who must be in a hospital for a long time need more than care by doctors and nurses. They need child care providers who will engage their minds. Qualifications for these positions depend on the age group with whom someone works. A college degree is usually needed for teaching older children.

Meet Stephannie

Stephannie Ledesma began working at Fairfax Hospital in Virginia as a volunteer. She then became a coteacher and finally a teacher. Although she is now a special education teacher in the public schools, she still volunteers at the hospital. Many young adults volunteer part-time, and she feels that working at a hospital as a staff member, whether volunteer or paid, is an excellent way to check out a career in child care.

At the hospital, Stephannie was a member of the Child Life staff. She supervised recreational activities and taught academics.

The goal of the Child Life staff was to interact with students in a nonmedical way. For example, they would teach math but then they would also play chess.

Although the job paid very little, Stephannie says it helped her gain special skills. Because the Child Life staff took students on field trips, nurses trained them in how to secure wheelchairs in a van, administer first aid and CPR, and work special medical machines.

Stephannie says there are three problems with such a job:

- Because pay is low, staff turnover is great. When people on staff leave, it can be hard for some of the children. The children see very few people other than those in white coats. If a child gets attached to a caregiver who then leaves, the child often suffers emotionally.

- Most of the children have severe health problems. They are not able to communicate well. Many are nonverbal, which means they are not able to speak. "The job can get frustrating," Stephannie says, "because there's no feedback from the kids."

- Many of the children can do little with their hands, so the caregiver must carry out most of an activity. The caregiver, for example, often has to do an art project. The value to the child is in seeing the process, touching the result, and feeling the texture.

73

Chances to move up the administrative ladder were possible, but Stephannie says, "Through this child care job, I realized I really like to teach and decided to get a degree so I could teach special education."

AFTERSCHOOL CARE

Afterschool care is one of the fastest growing areas in the child care field. The National School Age Care Alliance (NSACA) describes growth in this type of child care as "explosive."

The National Institute on Out-of-School Time reports that, in the United States, at least five million children between the ages of five and twelve do not have adult supervision after school hours. These long hours without an adult to oversee a child's activities can amount to twenty to twenty-five hours per week, they note. (See Appendix A for information on the National Institute on Out-of-School Time, Wellesley College Center for Research on Women.)

At best, this time allows children to spend after-school hours passively watching television. At worst, this time allows children to become involved in juvenile crime as either a victim or as someone who commits a crime. Because of concerns like these, a huge effort is being made to provide afterschool programs. Many of these programs are held in open areas of schools, such as gyms, or in community centers.

Today, afterschool programs are uneven in quality. Good ones provide options for the youngsters. They involve the children in fun activities in a caring, structured way that will lead them toward independence. After a full day of school, some children need quiet time to relax. Others need a place to exercise and play sports. Still others want to complete homework. Some want to do something creative, with arts and crafts. And yet others may want an older person to talk with them about a problem. Someone who works with children in an afterschool program would help them in all these kinds of activities. Depending on the activity, you could be a friend, teacher, mediator, guide, leader, or participant.

Jobs caring for children under the age of twelve offer variety. Such jobs may lead to a satisfying career or could be a springboard to a different career.

10

Administrative Positions

Typically, child care workers who want a new challenge move into administrative positions such as director or assistant director of a center. Some decide to become an owner or owner/director of their own center. For many teachers, this is a logical move that allows them to remain in the field of child care.

NEW CHALLENGES

Even if an administrative position in the child care field seems like a natural step, these jobs involve taking on a role that is very different from work in the classroom. A director must take a broad view of the school and its program. When asked what she felt the most important part of her job is, Carol Corbett, the director of WEE Center in Rockville, Maryland, replied that directors have to ask themselves:

- What can I do to make the school a good place for someone to work?

- What can the school offer to the staff that makes them want to stay?

Many directors seek to improve the salaries of their staff. But salary, since it depends on fees paid by parents, cannot be raised so high that the weekly cost to parents is extreme. Other ways to improve staff morale and help the employees to enjoy their jobs need to be found.

Some of the benefits directors can provide, Carol told us, are tangible. These include having staff lunches and giving a gift or bonus at Christmas.

Administrators can pay for a teacher to attend a class, a conference, or a workshop. They can also start a library of current professional books and magazines. Such steps build morale and help staff become better child care providers.

Other benefits that encourage staff, such as affirming someone's good work, are intangibles. According to Carol , directors need to know what staff members are doing and commend them for their efforts. They must make staff "feel good about themselves and where they are." That means they have to keep their office door open for staff visits. They must also visit the areas—classrooms, playground, and lunchroom—where staff and children spend their day.

MOVING OUT OF THE CLASSROOM

Only you can decide if you prefer to work directly with children or if you will enjoy a job out of the classroom.

Someone who moves into administration faces many challenges. One of these involves communicating with parents, staff, children, and people in the community on a daily basis. This contact ranges from pleasant, routine meetings to encounters that can be very hard to handle.

While interacting with people is a big part of the work of a director or other administrative support person, other duties make each day different.

MEET BONNIE

Bonnie Redmond is the owner/director of Community Montessori School (CMS) in Herndon, Virginia. Although Bonnie's work is oriented to the Montessori approach to learning, most of what she does during the day is what a director of any child care center does.

Each day is full. Bonnie generally oversees the daily routines of the school and handles lots of jobs. "At twelve noon, I'm a nurse," she says. "At 4:00 PM, I'm a maid, and at midnight I'm a bookkeeper."

Mondays are especially hectic. Bonnie starts the day by cleaning the playground of debris from weekend functions at the church where the school is located. Then she checks each teacher's lesson plans and approves the outline of what they will do during the coming week. She also prepares a newsletter for parents.

Other days are almost as busy as Mondays. Staying in touch with parents takes a great deal of time. Accident reports for even minor mishaps are written up, and a copy for the parent is put in the child's "cubby." Of course, serious mishaps or sudden illness means immediate parent involvement. She also tries to help families through difficult times, such as moving to a new house or coping with the loss of a parent's job.

Bonnie spends time disciplining students when it's needed and acts as liaison between teacher and parent.

Reading is required every day to keep up with paperwork. Bonnie says, "Mail is endless. Changes of laws governing day cares and schools that are sent out by state social services for review and evaluation. Information about fundraisers. Ads of all kinds. The latest *Tomorrow's Child*." (*Tomorrow's Child* is a Montessori journal for teachers and parents.)

Paperwork also includes ordering supplies and materials, from playground toys to paper towels. "A huge amount of my time is spent ordering supplies," she says.

Other activities are not part of every week but take time when they appear in her appointment book. Bonnie is responsible for hiring and firing employees and for resolving conflicts that may arise between the staff members. She works hard to hire people who have personalities and skills that complement and mesh with those of existing staff members. She conducts periodic in-service training or educational sessions for her employees. Various state and local inspectors visit. She spends many hours in court as a witness in cases that don't involve the school but do involve parents and students.

Bonnie also tries to make the school part of the community. She takes prospective parents and visitors on tours of the school. She also acts as liaison with the larger community by attending town council meetings.

GETTING STARTED

Experience in the field of education, usually in child care, is necessary, in addition to some business experience or business courses. Bonnie's background within the field of education is typical. At age eighteen she began her career as a special education instructional assistant in a high school. Then when her own children were small, she worked at their Montessori school. She moved into a position as a teacher in a franchised child care center and then completed her training for Montessori certification.

Later she took a job in which the owner of a number of centers sent her to various schools to evaluate them. In judging the day-to-day functioning of each center and the attitudes of staff and their interactions with children and parents, she gained experience that was valuable in setting up her own school.

Salary Range

Salaries vary widely and are higher than salaries for teachers. In 1996 the Center for the Child Care Workforce conducted a survey for the California State Department of Education that found the median, or middle, of the salary range for directors of private for-profit centers was $18.83 per hour. In addition, 59 percent of the centers either fully or partly paid health care benefits. Teachers, on the other hand, earned $7.25 per hour and teacher assistants earned $6.43 per hour.

The same study found that directors of private not-for-profit centers earned a median salary of $14.30 per hour. (See Appendix A for information about the Center for the Child Care Workforce.)

The income for an owner/director depends on many variables, including location of school, rates charged at other centers in the community, and staff salaries. Some owners rent space; others buy the building and land on which the center is located. Obviously, acquiring a building and equipment requires a large initial outlay of funds.

Owning a school is not a way to get rich quickly. Someone thinking about owning their own school must also consider whether they want to spend the money, do the work, and experience the frustrations and risk involved in starting and running a business. The right building must be leased, bought, or built. To lease a space, time is needed to find the right location, settle the lease contract, and prepare the space to work as a school. Bonnie feels the risk, money, and time involved in starting her school were worth the effort. She says, "I love having my own business." She is rightfully proud of the job she has done at Community Montessori School.

TRAINING NEEDED

Most school directors and center owners have an associate or bachelor's degree. If they do not have a degree, they need teaching experience and a willingness to take classes for continued learning. Most states require continuing education credits each year for directors of a center. These courses include ones that improve teaching techniques and those that help directors run a small business.

Owning a school presents challenges that are more complex than those faced by a salaried director who handles only administration. Bonnie does not have a college degree, but she has an abundance of determination and organizational ability. She also has a spouse who supports her work and helps both professionally and at home.

MOVING OUT OF CHILD CARE AND INTO OTHER JOBS

Running a school is not a job for everyone. Some people want a challenge out of the classroom but do not want to become a director. For these people, work in child care provides the background for future work in many fields. Degreed teachers and other education professionals, such as college professors, therapists, and guidance counselors, often begin by working in child care.

"For eight years I was a teacher," says Deana Preston, a preschool resource specialist in Madison County, Alabama. "Now I am a specialist in my school system's preschool program. I complete intake info from parents, take referral info on the children, schedule testing, and serve as a representative in meetings for children with special needs. I am also working on a systemwide curriculum for the preschool special education teachers. And I hold parent workshops. I really stay busy."

MOVING INTO A PUBLIC SCHOOL SYSTEM

Because wages in the child care field are relatively low, even if you hold a college degree, most people who want to remain in the classroom decide to work in the public school setting.

"My child care years hold many, many special memories for me," says teacher Cindy Lenzi. "The sweetness, the silliness, the surprises, the honesty, the learning, the successes, and the freedom to be however I wanted to be because the children were never critical. But as I grew in experience and confidence, I wanted more authority, training, and money. I figured the best option that I had was to become a special education teacher. At times I still miss child care and think that I would like to be the director of a center, but I do enjoy the challenge of what I am doing, which is the job of head teacher in a special education classroom."

PART III

THE FUTURE

11

Your Career Start

If you have decided to pursue a career in child care, you're probably considering the position you'd like. You may even be checking ads in the local newspaper, talking to friends who may know of a job, and reading bulletin boards in the grocery store.

Because the demand is high for child care workers, you'll probably find lots of openings. But you may be unhappy if you rush to take just any job, and bouncing from job to job is not a great way to start a career.

The next three chapters will help you:

- Prepare yourself to find a job
- Find the job that is right for you
- Take the first steps in your new job

Much of the information is aimed at prospective teacher assistants and teachers, since most child care workers choose to work in a center. A great deal of what you'll read, however, also applies to those who choose home-based child care (nanny or family child care provider).

Use the checklist on the following page to consider the steps you should take before you begin to look for a job.

HAVE YOU SOUGHT OUT INFORMATION ABOUT CAREERS IN CHILD CARE?

In the back of this book, you will find contact information for child care groups and organizations all

Are You Ready to Begin a Career in Child Care?

☐ Have you sought out information about careers in child care?

☐ Do you know if you are right for this field?

☐ Are you absolutely sure that you want to work with children?

☐ Have you checked the requirements for child care workers in your area?

☐ Can you pass the required health and background checks?

☐ Have you asked people to act as references?

☐ Do you have a résumé prepared?

☐ Have you begun a portfolio?

☐ Can you verbalize your beliefs about child care?

over the United States and Canada (see Appendix A). Most of these have Web sites. Spend time seeking out additional information. Libraries are also a great source of books, magazines, and professional journals related to child care.

DO YOU KNOW IF YOU ARE RIGHT FOR THIS FIELD?

If you are presently enrolled in high school or a post–high school program, seek out the guidance department and ask if you can take some tests that will give you information about your abilities in the human services area. Talk honestly with a counselor about personal strengths and weaknesses, your skills, and if you have the right personality to work with children.

You can also find private companies that will, for a fee, counsel you in your career choice.

ARE YOU ABSOLUTELY SURE THAT YOU WANT TO WORK WITH CHILDREN?

When asked what advice she would give someone thinking about a job in child care, Michelle Belski, program coordinator at WEE Center, Rockville, Maryland, said, "Some people do this because they really want to and some because they want to have a paycheck. Don't do it unless you really want to. Kids deserve more and it's a hard, hard, hard way to make a living if you don't want to."

If you are sure a career in child care is what you want and your abilities and skills match those needed, you are ready to take the next steps to beginning your career.

HAVE YOU CHECKED THE REQUIREMENTS FOR CHILD CARE WORKERS IN YOUR AREA?

Part of the challenge of pursuing a career in child care is meeting the certification requirements. The federal governments in the United States and Canada do not regulate child care. States and provinces set their own standards, and requirements vary widely.

For example, consider training for what is called a senior staff job in Maryland. A senior staff person is someone in charge of a single group of children younger than age five. This job requires someone to be at least twenty years old, with a high school degree and six semester hours or ninety clock hours of approved training, plus one of the following:

- One year of college or a combination of college and experience that equals one year

- One year of supervised work experience in an approved setting

An associate (AA) degree in early childhood education is also accepted. With an AA degree the person must be nineteen years old. A third option requires a state department of education certification as a teacher, which essentially means you need a bachelor's degree from an approved college.

Travel a few miles north or west and the requirements change a great deal. Nearby Pennsylvania requires at least an AA degree in the field of education plus experience, or an AA degree in another field and thirty postgraduate credit hours in education. To qualify for a child care job, another neighboring state requires only that someone be eighteen years old, have earned a high school diploma or the equivalent, and be able to read and write.

The situation across Canada is as equally varied and hard to interpret. In 1996 the Child Care Connection in Nova Scotia pointed out, "At present, 'training' is defined by the Nova Scotia Day Care Act and Regulations as post–secondary Early Childhood Education training by an accredited institution, or a combination of accredited ECE training, experience, and non-accredited training."

You may have noted above that supervised work can often substitute for course work in fulfilling the requirements for a teaching job. Many teachers, even those who also take course work, elect to start their career as a teacher assistant, since the requirements for that job are often simply a basic high school education or the equivalent.

CAN YOU PASS THE REQUIRED HEALTH AND BACKGROUND CHECKS?

Most states and provinces require health and background checks. The health check includes immunizations and a test for tuberculosis.

Many areas now require a criminal background check and fingerprinting, even for volunteers. The school in which you work will often pay for this. If you have any sort of police record, describe and explain your situation at the time of your interview. It's always best to be honest and up front instead of explaining yourself once you have been checked out. A traffic ticket does not count as a criminal record. Traffic tickets may, however, impact on your being hired if part of the job involves driving children.

HAVE YOU ASKED PEOPLE TO ACT AS REFERENCES?

To get a job in child care, you will, as in most jobs, need references. Lining up references before you begin to look for a job is a good idea so that the people you ask will not be caught off-guard with a phone call or form to fill out.

If you are in high school or have recently graduated, a counselor or teacher is often willing to act as a reference. A leader at your place of worship, a neighbor, or someone who knows you well but is not a family member is also a good choice.

DO YOU HAVE A RÉSUMÉ PREPARED?

Before applying for a job, you will need to prepare a résumé that provides basic information about you. It doesn't need to be elaborate. A résumé will help a director remember you if other people are being interviewed for the same job. An attractive and organized résumé may give you an edge over the others. Plus, the director will have the information needed to reach you should he or she want to interview you.

You can find information about how to prepare a résumé in libraries or on-line. If you are in school, ask a guidance counselor or work coordinator for help and samples.

In addition to giving contact information, a résumé presents both someone's background and areas of strength. Think seriously about your strengths and make sure you present them in your résumé. For example, if you have taken a high school class in child development and a children's story you wrote won a prize from a local writing group, include that accomplishment.

HAVE YOU BEGUN A PORTFOLIO?

A portfolio is a notebook that shows you off as a professional. Even if you are just starting a career, you may have materials you can put in a three-ring binder and share when you interview. Include your résumé with an extra copy to leave with the interviewer.

The following are examples of items that will sell you and your skills:

- **Work samples.** If you have them, work samples are great to include in your portfolio. For example, if you taught a class at your place of worship and have a sample lesson you did, include that. If you substituted at a local center, include some drawings the students did. Work from a high school child development class is also a good addition.

- **Letters and notes that thank or commend you.** If you have a note from a parent for whom you baby-sat, add that. If you have done volunteer work or had a part-time job, ask for a letter of recommendation from the person for whom you worked.

Put any item that is a "one-and-only" in a plastic sleeve or use a photocopy of it.

Include in your portfolio any special papers that show you are capable and responsible. Don't be shy. Many people don't brag enough about themselves.

CAN YOU VERBALIZE YOUR BELIEFS ABOUT CHILD CARE?

Even if you have no training in the field, you have learned about and associated with young children in a variety of circumstances. You have observed children in your family and neighborhood. You have read this book and perhaps other books and articles about child care. You have seen movies, television programs, and news items that dealt with small children.

All of these and other experiences have given you feelings and ideas about the care young children should receive to help them develop and learn. For example, you may feel that children at age four should be given direct lessons in the letters of the alphabet and the sounds the letters make. Or you may feel that four-year-olds should be spending their day socializing with classmates and learning the alphabet only if they express a desire to do so. As a prospective professional, you should be able to say something about how you feel children should spend their day in child care.

This is not to say that how you feel today is how you will feel later in your career. Your own feelings and beliefs may change as you gain more experience. Classes or conferences will also help you refine your beliefs and perhaps change them. Nevertheless, when you apply for a job in child care, you should be able to tell the person who interviews you your beliefs about child care.

When you have taken care of the items on the checklist, you're ready to begin your job search.

12

Finding the Right Job

If you are going to work in a center, one of the most important steps you can take is to interview the director or another administrator. If you are going to work as a nanny, interview the parent (or parents) at the family's home.

Although that person will be interviewing you as well, you also need to conduct an interview of your own. Perhaps your interviewing will not be as obvious as the director's (or parent's) interview of you, but you still need to check out the place at which you may be spending many hours each day.

Terms appropriate for a job in a center—where most beginners apply—will be used in this chapter. If you are applying for a position as a nanny, substitute *family* for *center* and *parent* for *director* in the information that follows.

MAKING A GOOD MATCH
As you talk with the interviewer, you should consider how closely the beliefs of the center match your own.

While many centers do not promote any special philosophy, all of them have theories and ideas about caring for and educating young children. These are usually stated as goals and may be found in the center's "mission statement." This information is printed in a brochure or materials that explain their program. Goals may also be stated to you when you interview.

Meshing a center's beliefs about child care with your own is crucial to obtaining a job that you love to work at and one that also works for you.

DON'T TAKE THE WRONG JOB

The sad truth is that not all child care providers do a good job and not all centers provide good care. Edward Zigler is a professor of psychology at Yale University and is one of the founders of Head Start. At a 1999 conference, he said, "Children are in this system for five formative years and care is typically so poor as to compromise their social and cognitive growth."

Some authorities in the field feel that statements such as Zigler's are too strong. The Casey Journalism Center report "Covering Child Care and Early Learning," published in September 1999, notes that "others believe the impact of good child care is short-lived."

Even if authorities do not agree how much child care experiences affect adult life, most child care professionals agree that, all too often, children who cannot speak for themselves are harmed, or are open to harm, by poor care. This poor care can occur in many different ways, including:

- Physically harming a child

- Placing a child in a dangerous situation where harm can happen

- Putting a child's health at risk because of poor hygiene practices and poor quality food

- Emotionally abusing a child by yelling and humiliating them

MEET MICHELLE

Michelle Belski spent almost a year working in what she calls a "bad center."

The center was reasonably priced, so parents who were younger couples or young single mothers enrolled their children. Michelle said the parents didn't have experience with other centers that provided good care and had no way to compare the types of care children received. These young parents did not know how to ask tough questions about how the center was run and how the children spent each day. They were simply happy to have someone take care of their kids at a price they could afford.

Before long, however, Michelle heard and saw a lot of things that upset her. For example:

- Other staff members yelled at children and talked to them in a way that was demeaning.

- Children had no playground equipment. They simply ran around the playground area when they were outside.

- Many times teachers had responsibility for many more children than the state law allows because of staff absences with no substitutes.

- Lunch preparation caused a staffing problem and lunches were not nutritious. At noon a staff person was pulled out of a classroom to finish preparing lunch that had been started by a cook at 5 AM. The classroom was then understaffed. Menus were neither varied nor nutritious.

Michelle was worried that something might happen to a child. Not only would the horror of a hurt child affect her, but she was also worried the parent would sue her as well as the center. She stayed on for a while because she had developed a relationship with the children and felt they needed her. Finally, she says, "Being there for the kids wasn't good enough anymore."

Michelle also knew she could not count on the law to step in. Centers that violate the law are seldom reported. Inspections are few and in many places are scheduled so a center can thus prepare itself to look its best on its scheduled day.

Even if a center is found guilty of breaking the law, many states do not have immediate fines. A report on child care centers by the *Louisville Courier-Journal* newspaper revealed that because of the time and legal expense involved, Kentucky seldom attempts to shut down a center unless it feels that children are in danger. A case may drag on for years, and often the center stays open during that time. The situation may be better in some areas, but Kentucky is far from alone in not being able to respond quickly to problems in child care centers.

Michelle didn't want to get stuck in another bad center so she substituted for about a year. While substituting she found a number of good centers, but she found many that were poor.

By the time she interviewed at WEE Center in Rockville, Maryland, Michelle knew what to ask the director during the interview and what to look for as she toured the center. She recognized that WEE Center had the qualities of a good center she was seeking.

Learning about a Center Before You Accept a Job

CLEANLINESS, MATERIALS, AND EQUIPMENT
- ☐ Does the center seem clean?
- ☐ What are the routines for toileting and handwashing?
- ☐ Are many books, toys, and games available to children?
- ☐ Is there playground equipment?
- ☐ Does the playground look safe?
- ☐ Is the playground fenced in?

FOOD
- ☐ Who prepares meals?
- ☐ What are typical meals for a week?

ADMINISTRATION
- ☐ Is the director or another administrator always at the center?
- ☐ Is there a recommended series of steps for handling a student's difficult behavior?
- ☐ What are the backgrounds of the staff?
- ☐ What training opportunities, including in-service, are there for staff?
- ☐ How many staff usually leave each year?
- ☐ What is the student/staff ratio for the age group with whom you'll work?

CONTACT WITH PARENTS
- ☐ Is parent involvement encouraged through visits, newsletters home, phone calls?

CARING FOR THE CHILDREN (BASED ON YOUR OBSERVATION)
- ☐ What are your feelings about staff/child interactions?
- ☐ Do the children seem happy?

Hopefully you will not have Michelle's experience before you find a center that is the right place for you.

FIND ANSWERS DURING AN INTERVIEW

Just as parents spend a great deal of time finding the right child care placement for their child, you may have to spend a great deal of time before you locate a center that is a good match for you.

When you arrange an interview time, request that you interview when children are there and awake. If you visit after lunch or in the late afternoon, you will not be able to get a sense of how the children look, behave, and are treated by staff. You should be there when children are present and active.

If you feel you would like to work there after the interview, ask for a tour or for a time when you can visit and observe. If the director is serious about hiring you, he or she will usually agree.

WHAT TO LOOK FOR WHEN YOU VISIT THE CENTER

The checklist on the facing page is not meant to cover every possible fact about a center but can help you get a sense of what the center is like, both as you talk to the interviewer and as you observe when you walk through the halls. You may want to copy the checklist and take it with you.

You may not necessarily have to ask about the items on the checklist. During the course of the interview, the person who is interviewing you will probably talk about many of the items.

Often you will be asked at the end of an interview if you have any questions. Interviewers don't ask just to be polite. Most welcome intelligent questions. If you have not been told a salary, ask your other questions first and then ask about salary. You will appear more professional if you wait until the end to ask about salary.

Cleanliness, Materials, and Equipment

Consider the following questions:

- Given the time of day you visit, does the center seem relatively well maintained?
- Are toilet areas clean and stocked with soap and paper goods?
- Are there plenty of educational and fun toys for the children to play with and are they in good condition?
- Do staff seem prepared and attentive to the needs of the children?

Food Served

Prepared food may be delivered to the school, or the school may have its own kitchen. A published or posted menu can tell you how varied and nutritious the meals are. If you tour the facility, you can peek at where food is prepared and served. Are disposable products used? Does the area where dishes and utensils are stored appear clean?

Administrative Support

In the best centers, the owner, director, or staff member who serves as administrator is in the building and available at all times. Large centers may also have an assistant director, a program coordinator, or someone with a similar title. The title is not important to you, as a beginner in the field. What is important is that someone can be called on if a situation arises in which you need help or advice. This person should not be tied up with the daily, ongoing care of children for whom they are responsible.

Contact with Parents

A quality center should welcome parents into the building at any time. The center should also explain its program to them by sending home newsletters, making phone contacts, and having events at least several times a year. These events may be social or informative.

Caring for the Children

If possible, observe children in the classroom and on the playground. Consider the following questions:

- Are the children engaged in meaningful activities?

- Are the children smiling?

- Do they seem eager and excited about what they are doing?

- Are staff pleasant in their tone of voice and what they say?

- Does the staff treat the children warmly?

- Does the staff talk to the children in a way that validates them as worthy and respected?

- Do the children generally play happily with each other?

- Does the staff carry on their own private chats while they are working with children?

Michelle says, "I don't think how we talk to kids is stressed enough. Teachers will spend lots of time planning an art project but then talk negatively to students."

Still Not Sure?

You may come out of an interview with some of the questions on the checklist unanswered. Or you may have felt some of the things you were told conflicted with what you saw. If you are offered a position and are unsure if you should take it, ask if you can have several days to consider. If questions on your checklist went unanswered, you may want to address them again. However, if that is a problem for the prospective employer, you probably do not want to work there. When in doubt, use your intuition—the sense you have in the pit of your stomach that something is right or wrong for you. Intuition is often your best guide.

13

Beginning Your First Job

The first position in your chosen field of work is exciting. Unlike jobs taken only to earn spending money, working in child care means you are on your way with your career.

FIRST PRIORITY

Regardless of your job title or job description—nanny, family child care provider, teacher assistant, or teacher—your first priority as a child care provider is to ensure the safety and well-being of the children under your care.

As a child care provider, you'll need to learn the backgrounds of the children with whom you work. This information should include allergies, food likes and dislikes, family background, and anything else that may affect the well-being of the child. You'll also need to know each child's physical, emotional, and academic needs and strengths.

Document, or write down, anything out of the ordinary, such as an accident on the playground or bruises on the child. If you do not feel at ease writing, ask for help or use a tape recorder.

HOW TO DOCUMENT

Many child care programs have guidelines for reporting incidents and accidents and, if needed, letting parents know what happened. If a program does not stress documenting or if you are alone as a nanny or family child care provider, you should still keep notes. Trusting yourself to remember doesn't protect the child or you; thorough notes can remind you and serve as proof of what happened and the results of care that was given.

A written record is best but a tape recording is better than neglecting to document. Whether you are writing or talking on tape, give your name and the date first. Then explain the situation as clearly and fairly as you can. Don't make statements that refer to children in a negative way, like "The child is a terror on the playground." Avoid making judgments such as "Janie doesn't like Sam so she hit him," or "Tina's bruises were caused by someone hitting her."

Take the view of a detached observer, even if you were very much part of the action. Here is a sample of an objective write-up:

> *Nov. 20, 2000. Report by Tashya Williams. This morning while she was hanging up her backpack, I noticed three bruises, each about the size of a quarter, on Tina Kemp. Two were on her right leg and one on her left leg. I called over Mr. Young and told him what I had seen. Mr. Young then asked Tina how she got the bruises since we had not noticed them yesterday. Tina shrugged and said her dog knocked her down when she was playing with him. Tina asked if she could go back to playing with the blocks. We said she could.*

A BASIC CURRICULUM

After basic health and safety needs are assured, what curriculum will you follow? If the place where you work does not have a standard curriculum you need to follow, here is one from Sydney Gurewitz Clemens, an education consultant and writer. It stresses the use of a question that will act as a curriculum theme.

For the teacher:

- How can I find out what will challenge these children?

- How can I show the children and their parents that they are growing and learning?

- How can I make the best use of time for a relaxed, explorative, creative program?

For the children:

- How can I best play with others?

- How do we find things out?

- How can I make a friend?

- What's going on with my body?

- What can we see growing every day?

- What can we make with blocks, cardboard, clay, paint, wire, and other art materials?

ACTIVITIES TO CARRY OUT YOUR CURRICULUM

Once you have a theme to engage the children, activities are needed to carry out that theme. Introducing good books to the children is one activity that all experienced care providers endorse.

Sydney Gurewitz Clemens stresses reading and writing. "Books, books everywhere," she says. Clemens recommends you have lots of paper and writing tools for scribbling and drawing letters.

Clemens's ideas don't stop with reading and writing. "Singing and singing and singing," she says. "Making up songs about what children are doing. Honoring the songs children make up as they work. Playing songs over and over that appeal to the children (try folk music and music from many different cultures, especially cultures that are represented in your center).

"Nursery rhymes aren't all equally child-friendly, so be thoughtful about the content. 'One, Two, Buckle my Shoe' is just fine and incorporates counting to ten. It can be treated as a choral experience, with one group saying the number lines and the other saying the rhyming lines, with the teacher conducting so sometimes it's soft and sometimes it's loud. Any four-line poem can be said repeatedly with children and they will learn and enjoy it. When the children have been playing hard and are huffing and puffing, I like:

Sometimes, when I skip or hop

Or even when I'm jumping

Suddenly, I like to stop

And listen to me, thumping. (Put the hand on the heart to feel the thumping as it happens.)"

DEALING WITH DISCIPLINE

The best way to deal with discipline problems is not to have them. Of course, that is not always possible. Sooner or later, one child will fight with or harm another child.

One of the best ways to minimize problems, however, is to plan in advance. Advance planning means to write lesson plans and then be organized and ready to carry them out. If you do not have the materials you need before you start a lesson, you risk losing the children's interest and attention while you scurry around collecting needed items.

If your center does not provide plans for you to use, look on the Internet and go to the library for books and magazines that you can use to write your own plans.

Written lesson plans are needed for all academic lessons. A good lesson plan has six parts:

- Goals

- Materials needed

- Activities, including changes to help children with special needs succeed

- Wrap-up

- Planned evaluation of children's learning

- Self-evaluation (done after the lesson)

You can use a variety of formats in writing your plan. There is an example of a lesson plan in Appendix B. Try using it and modify as needed to create the best plan for you.

BE CONSISTENT

Being consistent in the classroom will also avoid problems. Consider the following:

- Have a regular schedule so everyone knows what to expect, but be flexible enough to make changes if an activity isn't working.

- Let children know exactly what is expected of them.

- Always be polite, even when you're feeling grumpy or upset. Don't yell or use language you don't want to hear the children use.

- Note the good work of a child or of a coworker. Praise a job well done.

- Use quiet cues and gestures. Stand close to a wiggly boy. Use a secret gesture between you and the girl who chats too much to remind her to stop talking. Keep only three shirts or smocks at the art table. Disturbances will be less if only a few children work on a messy activity at one time.

FIND A MENTOR

A mentor is an older, more experienced person who is willing to help a younger, less experienced person become prepared for all aspects of his or her new job.

Try to find a mentor in your school or among the people you know. Hopefully it is someone who has or has had a job similar to your own or is currently working in a position that you aspire to so that he or she can offer help, give you ideas, and listen to your problems.

INVOLVE PARENTS

Invite parents to be a partner with you in their child's progress. Share information when they drop off or pick up a child. Send home notes and phone with good news; don't wait until a problem surfaces.

Children will realize you are working with their parents to provide a caring place where they like to spend the day.

PLEASE NOTE

No job is harder than a job in education. The road to being a master child care provider takes time. Remember that self-preservation is a necessary step.

The energy needed to work all day with small children requires that you take care of yourself. The following are some suggestions to keep yourself in good shape:

- Get the amount of sleep you need each night.

- Exercise at least three times a week or several minutes every day.

- Eat regular meals.

- Take time to be with friends or talk to them on the phone.

- Spend some time each day in a task that is fun and that is not related to children.

- Don't take on the problems of the children for whom you provide care.

- Don't be too hard on yourself. No new job is easy. Working with children is certainly very taxing and difficult.

Once you feel at ease in your new job, you can begin to think about refining and polishing your job skills, about collaborating with other staff, about more actively involving parents, and about seeking out new ideas the children will love. Before you do those things, though, stop a minute and give yourself a pat on the back. You are finding success in a rewarding career.

Glossary

active learning   Hands-on activities that encourage children's involvement and interaction.

cardiopulmonary resuscitation (CPR)   A procedure used to revive the heart when it stops beating.

center   (1) A place where children are given group care. (2) A special area of the classroom where a learning activity is located; for example, a writing center, art center, computer center, housekeeping center, etc.

certification   Endorsement by a state or province of a person's qualification for a position (teacher, director, senior staff, etc.).

circle time   The time when children sit in a circle for a lesson.

collage   A combination of materials of various textures and types pasted onto a surface.

curriculum   A program framework that describes what children are supposed to learn.

Developmentally Appropriate Practice (DAP)   Learning activities geared to a child's stage of development.

director   The administrator in charge of a center.

educationally appropriate   Learning activities geared to the age of a child.

family child care provider   Person who provides care in their own home for one or more children.

free play Time allowed to play with the toys, games, or books of the child's choice.

Head Start A federal government program for children between the ages of three and five from families that meet poverty guidelines.

inclusion Term used to describe including children with disabilities into regular education programs and activities.

license A document given to a center or family provider if standards for performance are met.

median Middle of a range; for example, in the range of numbers from one to nine, five is the median.

nanny Person who lives in or out of the family home; does household chores related to child care but main job is to care for children.

peer Someone who has an equal ranking with another person.

portfolio A binder someone prepares to show samples of his or her work.

senior staff A certified teacher in charge of one group of children.

tutor One who instructs or teaches someone individually.

unregulated Not subject to laws and rules.

Appendix A: Information about Child Care Organizations and Training Programs

In the first part of Appendix A, you will find a list of child care groups and organizations in the United States and Canada. You can contact them for further information about the child care field. Selected programs that offer course work and training in the field of child care are found in the second part of Appendix A.

GROUPS AND ORGANIZATIONS

Some of the organizations, such as the National Association for the Education of Young Children (NAEYC), the largest child care organization in the United States, offer a great deal of general advice and material. Others provide special information; for example, the Center for the Child Care Workforce has information specifically related to training, salary, benefits, and betterment of the profession.

Using the Internet

Using the Internet is the quickest and cheapest way to access information. Keep in mind that while the Internet gives easy access to a wealth of material, Web sites often change and are often not totally up-to-date.

Sometimes, only a Web site appears below as contact information. A mailing address or telephone number often does not exist. In those cases, a group of partners probably united to sponsor the site.

A more extensive list of organizations in the United States than appears below can be found on-line at the National Child Care Information Center at www.nccic.org. In Canada, a list can be found at Child and Family Canada at www.cfc-efc.ca (then click on "View List of Partners").

In the United States

American Montessori Society (AMS)

AMS serves as a national center for Montessori information, both for its members and for the general public.

281 Park Avenue South, 6th Floor
New York, NY 10010-6102
(212) 358-1250
Fax (212) 358-1256
Web site: http://www.amshq.org

Association for Childhood Education International (ACEI)

Supports education and development of children and professional growth of educators worldwide.

17904 Georgia Avenue, Suite 215
Olney, MD 20832
(301) 570-2111 or (800) 423-3563
Fax: (301) 570-2212
Web site: http://www.udel.edu/bateman/acei

Center for the Child Care Workforce

Works to improve child care services by promoting increased pay, benefits, and training of care providers.

733 15th Street NW, Suite 1037
Washington, DC 20005
(800) U-R-WORTHY or (202) 737-7700
Fax: (202) 737-0370
E-mail: ccw@ccw.org
Web site: http://www.ccw.org

CLAS Early Childhood Research Institute

The Early Childhood Research Institute on Culturally and Linguistically Appropriate Services (CLAS) is a resource bank of materials for use with students who are different with regard to language, culture, and disabilities.

University of Illinois
61 Children's Research Center
51 Gerty Drive
Champaign, IL 61820
(217) 333-4123
Fax: (217) 244-7732
V/TTY: (800) 583-4135
E-mail: clas@uiuc.edu
Web site: http://clas.uiuc.edu

Early Head Start (EHS)

A federally funded community-based program for low-income families with infants and toddlers, and pregnant women.

Web site: http://www.ehsnrc.org

ERIC Clearinghouse on Elementary and Early Childhood Education (ERIC/EECE)
Excellent source for reference materials. Publishes digests that give brief overviews of many topics in education.

Web site: http://ericeece.org

Head Start
Head Start is a child development program that has served low-income children and their families since 1965. Head Start and Early Head Start are comprehensive programs that serve children, birth to age five, pregnant women, and their families. Overall goal is to increase school readiness of young children in low-income families. Web site has list of regional offices.

Web site: http://www2.acf.dhhs.gov/programs/hsb

High/Scope
High/Scope's curriculum is research-based and the High/Scope Foundation is known for study in the field of early learning.

600 North River Street
Ypsilanti, MI 48198-2898
(734) 485-2000
Fax: (734) 485-0704
E-mail: info@highscope.org
Web site: http://www.highscope.org

International Nanny Association (INA)
The International Nanny Association serves as an information source for nannies as well as parents,

nanny agencies, and others involved with in-home child care. Publishes annual directory of training programs, placement agencies, and special services.

900 Haddon Avenue, Suite 438
Collingswood, NJ 08108
(856) 858-0808
Fax: (856) 858-2519
E-mail: dirina@aol.com
Web site: http://www.nanny.org

Montessori Foundation
A not-for-profit organization dedicated to advancing Montessori education. Offers information for anyone interested in learning more about Montessori education.

17808 October Court
Rockville, MD 20855
(800) 655-5843
Fax: (301) 840-0021
E-mail timseldin@montessori.org
Web site: http://www.montessori.org

National Association for Family Child Care (NAFCC)
Professional organization for family child care providers.

525 SW 5th Street, Suite A
Des Moines, IA 50309-4501
(515) 282-8192
Fax: (515) 282-9117
E-mail: nafcc@nafcc.org
Web site: http://www.nafcc.org

National Association for the Education of Young Children (NAEYC)

The NAEYC is the United States's largest organization of early childhood professionals. Membership in 1999 included a national network of more than 400 local, state, and regional early childhood organizations.

1509 16th Street, NW
Washington, DC 20036-1426
(800) 424-2460 or (202) 232-8777
Fax: (202) 328-1846
E-mail: naeyc@naeyc.org
Web site: http://www.naeyc.org

National Child Care Information Center (NCCIC)

The NCCIC, supported by the U.S. Department of Health and Human Services, promotes links between child care providers and groups, and supports quality services for children and families. It is sponsored by the Child Care Bureau.

To find out the requirements for a family child care provider or for child care positions, go to the NCCIC Web site and click on "State Profiles."

243 Church Street, NW, 2nd Floor
Vienna, VA 22180
(800) 616-2242
Fax: (800) 716-2242
TTY: (800) 516-2242
E-mail: info@nccic.org
Web site: http://nccic.org

National Head Start Association
Represents parents and staff to advocate for Head Start children, families, and programs. Publishes a quarterly journal and uses its national voice to inform and educate on behalf of children.

1651 Prince Street
Alexandria, VA 22314
(703) 739-0875
Fax: (703) 739-0878
Web site: http://www.nhsa.org

National Institute on Out-of-School Time
Sponsored by Wellesley College. Works to improve the number and quality of programs for children during hours they are not in school.

Center for Research on Women
Wellesley College
106 Central Street
Wellesley, MA 02481
(781) 283-2547
Fax: (781) 283-3657
Web site: http://www.wellesley.edu/WCW/CRW/SAC

National Network for Child Care (NNCC)
The NNCC is a network of colleges and universities, sponsored by the Extension Office of the United States Department of Agriculture (USDA).

Web site: http://www.nncc.org

National School-Age Care Alliance (NSACA)

NSACA, with over 6,000 members in forty-seven states, reflects the diversity of the school-age child care field. Is an umbrella organization that supports quality programs for school-age children in their out-of-school hours.

1137 Washington Street
Boston, MA 02124
(617) 298-5012
Fax: (617) 298-5022
E-mail: staff@nsaca.org
Web site: http://www.nsaca.org

Reggio Children USA

For information about Reggio Children publications:

Office for Publications
c/o Council for Early Childhood Professional Recognition
2460 165th Street, NW
Washington, DC 20009
(800) 424-4310
Fax: (202) 265-9161

In Canada

Canadian Association for Young Children (CAYC)

The CAYC is a Canadian association concerned with the well-being of children from birth through age nine at home, in preschool, and at school. Members include parents, teachers, caregivers, administrators, and students. Publishes the journal *Canadian Children* and conducts conferences for those involved in early childhood education.

612 West 23rd Street
North Vancouver, BC V7M 2C3
Phone and Fax: (604) 984-2861
E-mail: info@cayc.ca
Web site: http://www.cayc.ca

Canadian Child Care Federation

Works to improve the quality of child care services for Canadian families by networking and communication. Publishes a quarterly magazine and resource sheets on a variety of topics of interest to parents and caregivers.

383 Avenue Parkdale, Suite 201
Ottawa, ON K1Y 4R4
(800) 858-1412 or (613) 729-5289
Fax: (613) 729-3159
Web site: http://www.cfc-efc.ca/cccf

Child & Family Canada

Child & Family Canada provides links to forty-six not-for-profit organizations that sponsor the site. Web site also provides articles on a variety of topics, available through an easy-to-use search engine of the site.

Web site: http://www.cfc-efc.ca

Child Care Resource and Research Unit

Resource for information about child care in Canada. A copy of the report "Flexible Child Care in Canada," is available from the address below or on-line at http://www.childcarecanada.org/download/flex.doc.

Centre for Urban and Community Studies
University of Toronto
455 Spadina Avenue, Suite 305
Toronto, ON M5S 2G8
(416) 978-6895
Fax: (416) 971-2139
E-mail: CRRU@chass.utoronto.ca
Web site: http://www.childcarecanada.org

Voices for Children
A Web site that specifically addresses Canadian child care issues and that offers a wealth of information for anyone interested in child care.

3 Rowanwood Avenue
Toronto, ON M4W 1Y5
(416) 408-3028
Fax (416) 408-3832
E-mail:voices@voices4children.org
Web site: http://www.voices4children.org

COURSE WORK AND TRAINING

Since more training often means more job opportunities and more pay than someone without training, anyone considering a career in child care should also consider course work. In addition, studies have shown that children directly benefit from having a teacher trained in early childhood education.

Many local colleges, including community colleges, and universities, provide course work and training in early childhood education. Classes taken through programs at colleges and universities are generally credit courses in terms of semester hours, which means a three-credit course meets approximately three hours per week for fifteen weeks, for a total of forty-five clock hours. Classes taken from child care associations and noncredit college courses usually measure courses in terms of the actual clock hours for which the class meets.

The following list of selected programs available in the United States and Canada provides useful information, including comparing programs for content, cost, and practical use to you.

Early Childhood News

Continuing education units and training hours are available from the University of Wisconsin-Stout through the professional journal *Early Childhood News*.

(800) 933-2829
Web site: http://www.earlychildhood.com

ECE Training Network

Students read content provided by ECE Training Network and material from links with pertinent information on the Internet. They have a message board dialog with an instructor and other students enrolled at the same time. Students who want a certificate for clock hours take a quiz that covers the readings and the interaction.

Web site: http://www.ecetraining.net

English Nanny & Governess School

30 South Franklin Street
Chagrin Falls, OH 44022
(800) 733-1984 or
(440) 247-0600
Fax: (440) 247-0602
Web site: http://www.nanny-governess.com

North Seattle Community College, Early Childhood Education Program

Offers a vocational program to gain an associate of applied sciences (AAS) degree in early childhood education. Courses stress practical teaching methods, with experience in the college Laboratory Preschool. Also available:

- Specialty certificate in child care directing, covering the managerial, financial, personnel, and business side of early childhood education.

- Paraeducator speciality certificate for those working in non-certificated educational positions with special needs populations of any age.

Child and Family Education Division
North Seattle Community College
9600 College Way North
Seattle, WA 98103-3599
(206) 527-3798
Fax: (206) 527-3715
Web site: http://nsccux.sccd.ctc.edu/~eceprog

Ryerson Polytechnic University, School of Early Childhood Education

Offers a full- or part-time program that leads to a bachelor of applied arts in early childhood education degree.

350 Victoria Street
Toronto, ON M5B 2K3
(416) 979-5000
Fax: (416) 979-5239
Web site: http://www.ryerson.ca/ece

Wheelock College
The Center for Career Development in Early Care and Education works with other child care and governmental groups to influence program and funding and improve the quality of early childhood development. Training courses are offered at the college and field locations.

200 The Riverway
Boston, MA 02215
(617) 734-5200, ext. 211
Fax: (617) 738-0643
E-mail: centers@wheelock.edu
Web site: http://ericps.ed.uiuc.edu/ccdece/ccdece.html

Appendix B: Sample Lesson Plan

Toes—A Lesson Plan

Date 9/7/01

Goals:

- Review concept of right/left.
- Teach the children the main parts of a foot: heel, toes, toenails, sole.
- Help the children understand that sounds make up language (phonemic awareness).
- Help the children discover what they can use their toes to do.

Materials Needed:

Book, *Hello Toes! Hello Feet!* by Ann Whitford Paul (DK Publishing, Inc.)

Outline drawings of foot from side and from top, with parts labeled

Crayons
Chart paper and markers
Pencils (short)
Scrap paper

Activities:

1. Give children drawing of a foot to color.
2. Discuss parts of foot.
3. Children take off shoes and socks and point to each part of their right foot. Then they do same with left.
4. Talk about words that rhyme with different parts of the foot: heel/feel, toes/close, nail/sail, etc.
5. Ask what they can do with their toes.
6. Read *Hello Toes! Hello Feet!*
7. Ask for things not described in the book that they can do with their toes. Remind them of warm-weather activities. Encourage naming things that they don't like to happen when they are barefoot. Make a web of their answers on chart paper.
8. Have children take turns walking on heels and then on toes. Then have everyone march in a circle, first on heels and then on toes. Provide children with short pencils.
9. Show children how to put pencil between big toe and next toe. Have them make marks on paper. [Help Tami with this.]

Wrap-up:
Tomorrow we'll start by playing another rhyming game.

Evaluation of Learning:
Before putting shoes and socks back on, everyone point to various parts of their right foot. Check who has trouble.

Self-evaluation:
This lesson took longer than I planned. I need to break this into two or more lessons, add other activities. Would be good idea to invite a podiatrist to talk about foot care next year.

For Further Information

BOOKS

Bowman-Kruhm, Mary, and Claudine Wirths. *Everything You Need to Know About Learning Disabilities.* New York: The Rosen Publishing Group, 1999.

Clemens, Sydney Gurewitz. *The Sun's Not Broken, a Cloud's Just in the Way: On Child-Centered Teaching.* Mt. Ranier, MD: Gryphon House, Inc., 1983.

Eberts, Marjorie, and Margaret Gisler. *Careers in Child Care.* Lincolnwood, IL: VGM Career Horizons, 1994.

O'Connor, Barbara. *Mammolina: A Story about Maria Montessori.* Minneapolis, MN: The Lerner Publishing Group, Inc., 1993.

Reeves, Diane Lindsey. *Child Care Crisis: A Reference Handbook.* Denver, CO: ABC-CLIO, Inc., 1992.

Weiser, Margaret G. *Infant/Toddler Care and Education.* New York: Macmillan Publishing Co., 1991.

Yeiser, Lin. *Nannies, Au Pairs, Mothers' Helpers—Caregivers: The Complete Guide to Home Child Care.* New York: Vintage Books, 1987.

OTHER RESOURCES

Sydney Gurewitz Clemens

Sydney Gurewitz Clemens, M.A., is an early childhood educator, workshop facilitator and author.

73 Arbor Street
San Francisco, CA 94131
(415) 586-7338
E-mail: teacher@slip.net
Web site: http://www.slip.net/~teacher

Mommy's Biz
A comprehensive Web site for both parents and professionals. Provides links to child care sites of all kinds. Has curriculum articles and information. Offers an on-line newsletter.

Web site: http://www.mommysbiz.com

Teaching Strategies, Inc.
P.O. Box 42243
Washington, DC 20015
(800) 637-3652 or 202-362-7543
Fax: (202) 364-7273
E-mail: info@teachingstrategies.com
Web site: http://www.teachingstrategies.com

Montessori Connections
A Web site that leads to everything anyone could want to know about Montessori method, schools, materials, etc.

Web site: http://www.montessoriconnections.com

Index